Eric

Life is Extraordinary

Don't Miss it!

It's an

EXTRAORDINARY
LIFE

Don't Miss It

AVIVA
PUBLISHING
NEW YORK

RANDALL BROAD *and*
JUNE GRUSHKA-ROSEN, M.ED.

IT'S AN EXTRAORDINARY LIFE - *Don't Miss It*

Address all inquiries to:

www.ItsAnExtraordinaryLife.com

ISBN: 978-1-935586-09-8

Library of Congress Control Number: 2010922741

Editor: Tyler R. Tichelaar, Ph.D.

Cover Design & Interior Layout: Fusion Creative Works, www.fusioncw.com

Printed in the United States of America

For additional copies, visit: www.ItsAnExtraordinaryLife.com

DEDICATION

For Emily and Riley

BETTERING THE NEXT GENERATION

Somewhere along the line, some wise philosopher pontificated that it was the duty of every generation to better the next. This being the case, I have failed miserably since my dad set the bar so high I couldn't possibly surpass it with my meager existence. That said, my son has little challenge before him to accomplish such a feat.

CONTENTS

....

WAKING UP

....

WHEN ONE MAN, FOR WHATEVER REASON, HAS THE
OPPORTUNITY TO LEAD AN EXTRAORDINARY LIFE, HE HAS
NO RIGHT TO KEEP IT TO HIMSELF.

— JACQUES COUSTEAU

In March 2008, my eyes were opened to a new perspective and life took on a whole new meaning. In that month, I was diagnosed with Stage 3 Lung Cancer. Once the reality of this news settled in, my first emotion was to cry. Then I woke up from my first reaction of fear to begin an entirely new and uncharted journey.

To set the record straight, this book is not about cancer or the ramifications of being afflicted with it. Plenty of good books have already been written on that subject; however, it is important to note that cancer is an important undercurrent in these pages because without its appearance on the scene, this book never would have been written.

You will probably be surprised when I make this next statement. Early on, I decided to choose cancer, rather than to let it choose me. I chose to live with it as opposed to dying from it. Wait, you say—you just told me this book isn't about cancer, but then you highlighted the subject on several fronts. Correct, I have. But again, I must stress that this book is NOT about cancer. It's about living an extraordinary life without waiting for something like cancer to open your door to living that life. As such, I'm highlighting cancer as the instigator. It took cancer for me to realize just how short life is, how important really living is, and then how to find the ability to share how life is extraordinary with the clarity that having this disease provides.

For me, this book is far more important than chronicling the challenges of *my* cancer. It's about *your* life journey and awakening *your* call to live your life and make it extraordinary in the process. In the more than fifty years I have lived, I have witnessed over and over that making life extraordinary is more the exception than the rule for most people. In fact, I strongly believe that while having an extraordinary life could be almost ordinary, most people choose to let it remain a rarity.

Yes, I realize too well that we all have to make a living. But that doesn't mean we have to miss out on living in the process. Therefore, this book is designed from start to finish to assist you, the reader, in living your dream and not someone else's. There is a big difference.

By sharing my experiences to the best of my ability, my aim is to ensure the reader learns from my mistakes (as well as my wins). In each and every chapter, I present a series of stories that provide more than one perspective.

My idea to write this book initially began when I asked my son and daughter what they would most like me to leave them if an unforeseen situation arrived and I wasn't on hand to give them my advice.

My daughter Emily immediately replied, "Dad, tell me everything you know about running a business. I know in my heart that someday I will run my own, so I need to know what you know since yours was successful." Okay, I thought, that will comprise about ten pages. But you're on—I'll do my best to share my experiences, good, bad, and in-between that moved me through my business life.

My son, on the surface the more sensitive of the two, asked, "What happened, Dad? Did you get bad news from the doctor today?" "No," I replied. "This is important and regardless of what's happening to me, I feel every parent (everyone for that matter) should take the time to write his or her story for posterity's sake and have it down for the world to witness." Rather than buy that explanation, he shut down so I had to wait and rephrase my approach for another day.

The next time I asked him, "Riley, what is it about me that you like most and if for some reason I wasn't around when you needed that one thing, what would it be?" This time he stopped, thought a moment, and responded with, "Dad, I love your stories about your life. You always have the best stories. If you could share some with me in your book, that's what I'd like to have."

So there you have it. A book about how to run a business combined with life stories. In the process, I'll attempt to sprinkle in living your dream in lieu of someone else's. That's the content of this book because like my children, I feel those are the most important ingredients I have to leave for future generations.

I've collaborated with my close and trusted friend, June Grushka-Rosen. She is a "how to live an extraordinary life" visionary in and of herself, and without her assistance, this book would only be half full. Her extractions and observations on the subsequent chapters are immeasurable. She brings the pure essence of the message into light and purpose for every topic. I am eternally grateful for her gifts of creativity and foresight, for I wouldn't have known where to begin without them.

About a year or so ago, this book began simply as a blog for me to chronicle my thoughts, subsequent cancer treatment, and progression. If you find yourself in a "less than good news situation," I cannot stress enough the usefulness of a personal blog site. It provides a convenient venue to document your situation as a resource for everyone so you don't have to explain yourself over and over. When one comes home from a long day of chemotherapy treatments, about the last thing you'll want to do is handle a series of calls to multiple listeners and relay the day's events...thus, blog. I also find it provides hope and support to others looking online who might be in similar situations. Sometimes I hear from strangers who read my blog—not a few end up becoming my friends.

About a year following diagnosis, I made a blog entry titled, "Live Your Life as Though You Have Cancer." It became Chapter One of this book because it is a cornerstone admission and an underlying thesis. My emphasis here is on attitude. I believe strongly that my positive attitude toward the disease has kept me alive longer than the doctors expected.

So what does all this mean to you, the reader, and what should you expect to garner from investing your time in reading and trying to understand what I have to share? I hope I will encourage you to think about your own life when you've run into obstacles or been jammed by adversity. How did you move through it? Are you overlooking the multitude of blessings in your life? How can you be more aware of them on a moment-by-moment basis? How do you live each and every day as if you only have that day to live?

These are questions I will help you to answer as a guide and mentor hoping to assist you to create a clearer window to your soul so you can make your life truly extraordinary. Throughout the book, June has prepared what we call "Mastery questions" and other mini-exercises to correlate with my stories and examples; we hope you will take the time to answer these questions for yourself to help guide you toward living your extraordinary life. We all possess the opportunity to live an extraordinary life. We only have one life to live, so it's important to live it to its fullest and make it extraordinary. Not for tomorrow, not next week, or next year, but today. You will come to know that the phrase, "Yesterday is history, today a gift, tomorrow a promise" is not just a saying, but a way to live your life. All we have is right now, and that's where this book will take you—to the present, and to the opportunity to show up and not miss it.

MASTERING YOUR EXTRAORDINARY LIFE

We need to accept that we won't always make the right decisions,
that we'll screw up royally sometimes—understanding that failure
is not the opposite of success; it's part of success.
— **Arianna Huffington**

While this book's stories may have been sufficient to motivate and inspire you to grab ahold of your extraordinary life, it was designed to create an eclectic experience for you by having its pages sprinkled with challenges to stretch you, fables, poems, and extraordinarily powerful and delightful quotes, and finally, Mastery Questions whose answers will increase your Work/Life satisfaction.

You are encouraged to write among the pages and use this book as a trusted friend that is there for you with advice and your best interests at heart as you master your own destiny and create your individual life lessons throughout the backdrop of your Extraordinary Life.

To begin the journey, the following Mastery Questions were created so you can take inventory of where you are, what is missing in your life, and what is needed to keep you from "Not Missing It" (Your Extraordinary Life). While you can certainly just read the book and enjoy Randy's many stories and benefit from the book, ultimately the question you must ask yourself is whether you want to have an entertaining reading experience, or do you want to learn how to have your own extraordinary life. The Mastery Questions will help you to focus so you can make that Extraordinary Life possible all the sooner. Your answers to the questions will enrich your understanding of yourself and your goals, provide you with insights needed for you to create the life you want, and finally, provide you with the ability to execute your dreams. So let's begin:

MASTERY QUESTIONS

Who are you? Consider the following in creating your answer.

What is most important in your life?

_____

_____

What is your deepest passion?

_____

_____

What is your life's purpose? If you don't know yet, what do you think you would like it to be?

_____

_____

What do you want that is missing from your life in the following areas?

Increased Health/Fitness

_____

_____

Personal Needs/Development

_____

_____

Time to enjoy my Family

_____

_____

Meaningful Relationships

_____

_____

Spiritual Connection

_____

_____

Peace/Forgiveness of Self or Others

_____

_____

Making a Difference/Contribution

_____

_____

Being Valued

_____

_____

Greater Success

_____

_____

Financial Security

_____

_____

How will you get there? (Don't consider the difficulty. Believe you can get there).

_____

_____

How will you hold yourself accountable? Consider the following:

- Take regular "inventory" of your desires and goals.

- Measure your results by clearly defining when and how you expect to see results.

- Take note if patterns in your daily routine have shifted with you gaining more Work/Life satisfaction due to a change in your daily activities.

- Enlist an "unofficial" advisory board (trusted friends) to keep you honest. Schedule regular meetings to measure your outcomes.

- Find a mentor or hire a professional Coach to keep you accountable to your specific desired results.

- We encourage you to come back and reconsider these questions and mark your progress regularly so you can see just how Extraordinary your Life will and has become.

We must overcome the notion that we must be regular...
it robs you of the chance to be extraordinary and leads you
to the mediocre.
— Uta Hagen

Chapter 1

....

LIVING LIFE AS IF YOU HAVE CANCER

....

It's not the years in your life that count.
It's the life in your years.
— Abraham Lincoln

If you found out today that you had cancer, imagine how your life would change. Step back for just a moment and attempt to contemplate the unimaginable. You are now at the beginning of a new and uncharted journey. Ask yourself, "How would my life change?" Would you begin to analyze your mortality with a more urgent sense? Would issues that seemed important become less so? Would subjects of top priority take on an even greater sense of urgency?

If you are like me and the multitude of cancer recipients around you, your view of life would change. You would live far more in the immediacy of the now. You might view life not so much from this world, but from a more eternal perspective. The next time you see your friends, you can't help but contemplate that it might be the last time you're with them in this world. When you go to a movie theatre with a friend or your son and daughter and watch the trailers for upcoming films and the release date is flashed before you, will you wonder whether you'll be alive to see the movie? What about the next holiday perpetually being planned wherever you look or listen? Will you be there to celebrate it?

Once the reality of cancer sets in, your fears change from a standpoint of doing to one of not doing. Imagine not living your life in fear for tomorrow, but alive today. Remember all those nights you lay awake thinking about the "ifs" of tomorrow and how important they were. Give some thought to how previously, there was always tomorrow, and how you made life harder than necessary by worrying about things from the view of "what if" and wondering what might be, what might happen as opposed to what is and the life before you this very moment.

At some time in your life, I'm guessing you've pondered the question, "If tomorrow were not an option what would you do today?" Be honest. Ask yourself the question now. Would you change anything? Would the world look different? Would you pick up the phone and tell a long lost friend or loved one something you've been meaning to say? Would you run to your kids' rooms and throw your arms around them and tell them how much you love them and how incredibly important they are to you? Would you do the same with your parents, your siblings? Would you be a different person? Would you view the world differently? Be honest.

Give this some deep and meaningful thought. Not from the negative or sadness point of view, but from a position of walking in cancer's shoes. Let the situation sink in, and think hard and deep about how your life would change. Think about life and how you can change your perspective from living for tomorrow to living for today.

Cancer has been a blessing for me in making me come to live for today. It has been and remains neither a curse nor a death sentence for me. Instead, it has been a window to living. Cancer has provided a very clear and fog free window from which to look on this world. It is also a daily reminder of just how short this trip is that we're on. Cancer, if you're open to the prospect of awakening, can give you a second chance.

I've come to understand death and that it is imminent for us all. None of us is immune. It's LIVING in this life that is hard. So to everyone who cares to listen, I challenge you to live fully. To live for today—not for tomorrow or some far off dream. Not in the seats as a spectator, but on the stage as the principal in a play.

Imagine you have cancer. Choose to live your life as such. You might be amazed at the possibilities that open up when you choose to be in this world with this point of view.

LIVING IN CANCER'S SHOES

Trying on "cancer's shoes" is not meant to be a dark task to send you racing down the road to put on your comfiest PJ's, crawl into bed, and stick your pillow up over your head. It is posed as a challenge to help you "wake up" to your life and discover or rediscover what is most important to you, what can no longer be put on hold, and what "old and new business" should be taken care of or brought to closure. And finally, it is meant to empower you to live each day fully and to embrace your Journey, ensuring that you "Not Miss It" (your Extraordinary Life)!

So try on "cancer's shoes" and embrace the challenge below. Stop to think it through, and then write down the answer.

MASTERY QUESTION

If tomorrow were not an option, what would you do today?

_____

_____

_____

_____

Consider the following in making your answer:

Would you change anything?

Would you treat people differently?

Would the world look different?

Remember to be honest.

Chapter 2

....

LEARNING FROM THOSE WHO KNOW

....

THE MORE I LEARN, THE LESS I KNOW.
—ANONYMOUS

When you're a teenager, few people if anyone can tell you more than you already know. After all, by that wonderful age there's little in the world you haven't experienced. My two teenagers remind me weekly how much I don't "get it." I guess as you get older, you know less.

When I was at the ripe old age of seventeen, I told my dad, "I feel like I've really got a good grasp on life and know what's what." He just looked at me and didn't say a word. Looking back, I find his silent response brilliantly appropriate; there obviously were no words sufficient for responding to my incredibly stupid moment.

Among my favorite of Mark Twain's witticisms is, "When I was seventeen, my dad was so dumb I could hardly stand to be in the room with him. And in four years time, I was amazed at how much he'd learned." That view certainly applied to me.

Being a teenager with hormones running amuck, I thought "fitting in" was about as high on the chart as it gets. And what I wore was imperative to accomplish the all-important aspect of finding my way. No matter whether it's at school, after school, on the weekend, in the evening, during basketball or while skiing or any other activity, what's on your back, legs, and feet is not to be taken lightly. Everything must conform yet be the latest that everyone else is wearing…no trail blazing here—that would be very, very "un-cool."

One day, I returned from a "must" shopping spree at the University Book Store and procured a pair of white cotton gym shorts with the really cool blue University of Washington logo on the front lower part of the right leg. These shorts were the bomb as all the cool guys in PE had a pair, and I was not about to be left on the sidelines waiting to be picked for sides without mine. I even bought a pair of matching blue with white logo. I was cool.

The shorts went straight in the wash to give them that "non-new" look. Once out of the wash, they went straight to the dryer. I couldn't wait to pack these babies off to school the next day and rock in Physical Education (PE)!

When I returned home from tearing about, my mom was busy doing her afternoon ironing. Hot on the board were my newly procured shorts. In dismay, I yelled, "What on Earth are YOU doing ironing my shorts?" As she looked incredulously at me and a bit bewildered, she passed the steaming iron across the most sacred of the sacred—the blue silk-screened University of Washington logo. After this quick pass, the face of those shorts was left with a blue smear stain. I went ballistic!

I was so angry I didn't even hear the exact words that escaped my mouth. But the ensuing rampage was so great it brought my dear mother to tears. Later, I would feel some shame for my uncontrolled outburst that ruined my mother's day, but at the moment, I could not stop my verbal assault. I stormed off with the ruined shorts in hand and tomorrow's expectation turned into a cloud of disappointment hanging overhead.

That evening, as I sat in the family room, my dad was in his casual chair with the accustomed *Seattle Times* opened across his lap. We said hello and asked how each other's day had been. He then asked me what had transpired to upset my mother so much. Being filled with righteous behavior, I spewed out my take on the disaster. I felt I had made a very good case, so much so that Perry Mason himself would have felt good about the cross-examination. My dad's only response was to ask, "How much did the shorts cost?" "Five dollars," I replied with indignant pride.

Once my diatribe had concluded, my dad calmly leaned forward in his chair, reached in his back pocket, pulled out his wallet, and extracted a crumpled up five dollar bill. He stretched his arm my way and said, "Here, son; here's five dollars. Go upstairs and make your mother cry again, and it's yours. After all, that's worth five bucks isn't it?"

In that moment, I realized that even I, a brilliant teenager, was outmatched. The feeling of being a complete imbecile consumed my adolescent self, leaving me with nothing left to say or do. I was completely bewildered and took my painful life's lesson with shame.

I don't know why I did it, I don't know why I enjoyed it, and I don't know why I'll do it again.
— **Bart Simpson**

By living your life every day as if you have cancer, you will most likely keep moments like this one from ever occurring. Your priorities will change as you realize what's really important, although being all knowing at an early age might get in the way. But let's hope and pray it doesn't.

LEARNING FROM THOSE WHO KNOW

When climbing ladders, swimming tides, brokering deals, entering or exiting relationships, buying homes, making parenting choices, or settling into college, it is difficult to know if we are making the right choices. Anxiety, frustration, and fear all color our ability to execute. Our emotions take over and we begin to "act out" or question our abilities.

Here are a few things to consider that will help to calm the mind and to replace apprehension or cockiness with confidence and sound decision-making:

Learn from those who know

- Acknowledge that you know nothing

- The smartest people are the ones who are willing to admit how little they really know.

Choose your attitude

- You are in-control of your attitude. Life is not happening to you without your consent.

- In order to find yourself, you must be willing to lose yourself along the way.

No single right answer

- There is always more than one right answer. Listen with your head, your gut, and your heart equally.

- Remember, most decisions can be renegotiated or revisited and rarely is anything preeminent.

Be a Chameleon

- Adapting to different environments is an essential survival asset. Be flexible and resilient as you learn to "drive" in any new territory. In addition, when assessing your final destination be open-minded. Remember, it takes a lifetime of trial and error to formulate who you are at the core, to "come clean" with yourself, and allow for your personal growth to be actualized.

Consequences

- With risks come consequences. Some will be challenging but most will be extraordinarily rewarding. Fasten your seatbelt!

MASTERY QUESTIONS

What life direction did you feel pigeonholed into, based on the strong influence or "agenda" of others?

_____

_____

What scenarios in your life were positively chosen based on intuitive guidance of others?

_____

_____

What activities, career choices, career goals, or ventures would you presently explore if you had no limitations?

_____

_____

Chapter 3

FALLING IN LOVE

I WAS NAUSEOUS AND TINGLY ALL OVER. I WAS EITHER IN
LOVE OR I HAD SMALLPOX.
— WOODY ALLEN

Being in love is one of the greatest experiences in life. Few things are more enjoyable than young, innocent love, and as lore will have it, the first love is the strongest. After all, it's the only time in life when you're in love and haven't yet had your heart broken. It's as intense an emotional sensation as there is, and it becomes permanently etched into your memory.

Love is bigger than physical attraction, beauty, great sex, or a *Leave it to Beaver* household. It's at an entirely higher level, and the only way you achieve that pinnacle of emotion is through time with the person you realize you cannot live without. It doesn't happen in a day, a week, a month, or even a year. It takes time. You have to seep into each other's very souls. And that takes time.

For me, the first time love happened was when I was twenty-two. I was in my first real work experience just out of college. I was toiling away at a job with which I was less than enamored. I dreaded getting out of bed each day to make the thirty-mile commute. Then, my sixth month there, my attitude changed. Sue arrived on the scene as our group secretary. She was all of nineteen, blonde, curvaceous, cute as cute can possibly be, and had a sense of humor and natural wit to match. She was a pistol with just enough vinegar to go with any greens a guy would ever want. I was smitten from the get-go.

Being the cock of the walk that I thought I was, I decided to play it cool with this one. No way was I was coming out of the chute letting this little hot blonde vixen think she was anything but. Silly me. She had me pegged from the moment she arrived, and she played me like a finely tuned fiddle, even though I had a couple of years more experience under my belt.

Back in these days, secretaries used typewriters and the best option to correct their mistakes was to use white-out. I didn't realize this at the time. When I appeared at Sue's desk with a make-believe request, she'd look up through her oversized glasses, and I'd notice she had white all over her fingers. I thought she was a painter on the side. Innocently, I'd ask how she was coming along with her part-time painting job. The only response I'd receive was to see her glasses steam around the edges of her nose. I had no idea about the effect that comment had on her at that tender age as it shook her workplace confidence—not to mention how I made her heart race as much as she did mine. Again, silly me—I let a couple of months go by with this flirtatious banter without coming clean about my true feelings.

Finally, I figured out a non-committal way for us to go out

together on a nonchalant date. Don't ask me the details of how I asked—they've left my memory. I just recall us tooling down Interstate 405 in my two-seater with the lid off, her sitting in the seat beside me and looking my way, smiling with her hair blowing around her face—and her underwear showing under her exposed skirt.

We ended up at a Lake Shore Park, on a summer night under the stars without a blanket, lying in the grass and embracing as only two people so infatuated with each other can do. It was a memory to behold and one I cherish to this day. The sweetness, innocence, desire, and connection we experienced was second to none. Best of all, it was mutual. That two people could possibly want so much from each other, on an equal footing and with so much bliss, was astonishing. God bless youth in perceived love.

We had so much fun…that's all I'll say to protect the innocent. Not a moment did I not enjoy being in her company. She made me laugh, smile, giggle, sweat, and pulsate. She raised my blood pressure to a state of ecstasy and anticipation for the next time we'd be together like no other woman could. She was it, and I thought about her every waking moment and in-between.

During the work-week, I couldn't wait for the final hour to end so we could make our way to my car and stay together until way, way after dark—talking, laughing, kissing, and just being in the immediacy of the moment. Just two people in love with being in love. It was wonderful on so many fronts and the feelings and emotions wrapped around my heart at the time were an explosion of passion and desire. She meant the world to me and never before had I experienced this level of loving sensation brought about by another person.

Then it ended as abruptly as it started. She had dated a long time boyfriend who fished in Alaska in the summers. Once he came back home, she tossed me back into the pond. It hurt. It really hurt. So much so I can't tell you. All I wanted was for her to come to her senses and realize what she was giving up. I knew in my heart that no one could make her happier than me, but I didn't have the skills to demonstrate it. Pride got in the way, and rather than take a risk and try to change her mind, I retracted and let him win without a fight.

My pride was too great to give her any room to make amends. After all, I was funny, young, smart (so I thought), affectionate, virile, but most of all, I knew I could be the most important person in her life forever. Looking back, my pride was foolish since like me, she was also young and searching. She did not realize my commitment to her, and now my pride would not let my full feelings be known. We both lost.

Now a new dynamic appeared—I had to deal with being around her at work on a day-to-day basis. It was hell. My heart was so heavy that I had difficulty functioning on any level. I was miserable, and being unable to control the feeling, it reflected on my productivity.

I've seen more than I care to share and heard plenty more horror stories of workplace romances. But at that tender age, my heart had been ripped out through my lungs. It didn't take Freudian analysis for me to learn a valued lesson. I swore I would never again mix work with pleasure, dip my pen in the company ink, crap where I ate, etc. No, I had received a deep and cutting warning. With plenty of fish in the sea, I had no need to pull my net from the company estuary. Nonetheless, my heart was splattered all over the exterior of my body, and I did everything possible to hide the mess so no one would see the hurt I was experiencing.

I'm not saying it's wrong to find love in the workplace, just dangerous. I'm sure many have succeeded. But I also believe that for everyone who has, ten more haven't. That's a bad ratio and it's merely subjective, but I'll bet my net-worth that my assumption is close to the truth. But, everyone is human, and if it's real, it's real, so you better go for it, not look back, and take all the risks you have in your bag of tricks to make it work. Otherwise, it's a dangerous play with only hurt and despondency as your reconciliation.

Even so, if I had to live it over again, I wouldn't change a thing. The good part is one of my greatest memories because for that short time, I was as happy as a man could possibly be. The old saying, "It's better to have loved and lost than never to have loved at all" most certainly applies.

Looking back, I can easily see why first loves affect us so powerfully. Because it's the first, the memory is baked into our brains with a vividness and clarity like no other, and the memories will not fade. Think back to other firsts in your life—your first day of school, first kiss, first sexual encounter, going away to college, or where you were and what you were doing when someone famous died and you heard the news. All are firsts and as such, solid memories you will not forget.

My experience with first love provided me with a lifelong impression on matters of the heart. It took a long time for me to work through my feelings about that relationship, and it heavily affected how I handled my relationships for many years thereafter. It embossed a stencil of experience upon me that

I played out again and again. I built a wall around my being (conscious or unconscious) that kept the opposite sex at arm's length from fear of being hurt so deeply again. The experience was so powerful that its effects were drastic upon my future relationships, and I know I'm not alone in how I allowed my first broken heart to make me defensive.

Even so, I'd still do everything again exactly the same way to experience that one time feeling and conjure up those heightened emotions. It was that good!

EXTRAORDINARY LOVE

One thing that makes Life Extraordinary is love. Life's greatest gift lies in our capacity to love, no matter the form of that love—finding romantic love, experiencing true love, raising children with our love, being there for our friends and neighbors through love and often most difficult, opening our hearts to self-love.

Love comes in so many complex and delicious flavors; too often it can leave us disappointed, heartbroken, and perplexed, yet so richly satisfied when we learn from our journey's trials and lead with an open, not closed heart. Yes, it's scary to trust that the world is generally out to do us good not harm. But closed hearts lead to less than ordinary days and being right does not always lead to happiness.

True extraordinary love comes in the form of understanding and respecting each other. So if we are brave enough to "give up" our own old destructive "stuff" long enough to open our hearts and reach across to another, that is where extraordinary love is experienced.

MASTERY QUESTIONS

Who in your life has represented a pure love experience for you at its highest potential? Name as many or as few people as feels accurate.

_____

_____

What was it that you gained from these individuals and how has that experience formed you?

_____

_____

How can you use these experiences to make the world a more extraordinary, loving place to live in?

_____

_____

Chapter 4

....

GETTING "LARRYED"

....

THERE IS NOTHING NOBLE ABOUT BEING SUPERIOR TO
SOME OTHER MEN. THE TRUE NOBILITY IS IN BEING
SUPERIOR TO YOUR PREVIOUS SELF.
— HINDUSTANI PROVERB

Every medium to large-sized organization has a Larry. He's the guy who comes from another company or an entirely different industry. Typically, he is hired under a new managerial team. It may take the better part of a year or so for him to appear on the new organizational chart, but know he's out there and his arrival is imminent.

Larry has no track record. Team members know little to nothing about him when he appears, and he sits on the sidelines very quietly, never looking his prey in the eye. When you do get the off chance to probe into his past, you'll get a non-committal answer issued from the corner of his mouth—some vague assertion about what he was responsible for, how much value he brought to his previous organization, and some seemingly amazing accomplishment that can never be verified.

Larry couldn't cut a deal or have an original thought if his life/career depended on it. Still Larry is vital to many an organization. You see—Larry is the hired gun. He rides in one day, makes his presence known, and then waits for the right moment to pull the trigger on his unsuspecting victims.

If you need a visual aide, watch the movie *Shane,* where the Larry character is played by Jack Palance, the hired gun who works for the local cattle baron to drive off the settlers who want to "fence in the prairie" and eliminate open grazing for their livestock. He arrives on a black horse complete with a black hat and double holster gun belt, his signature trademark. His spurs jangle as he strides down the wooden walkway in front of the town merchants. It isn't long after his arrival that he positions himself on a chair outside the swinging saloon doors with his hat tipped over his eyes to avoid any unsuspecting local target from making eye contact with him. But he knows exactly for whom he's aiming and the right moment to strike. And he's quick on the draw—he'll shoot his rival dead in the street before the challenger even knows what struck him.

That's the metaphor for Larry of the corporate world—the hired gun of upper management complete with a black suit and briefcase–who strolls into the office one day with the sole purpose of weeding out the chaff and doing the new regime's dirty work so his bosses won't have to get their hands dirty. Larry is the insulator who keeps the upper echelons away from the unpleasantries of corporate clean-up, either because they don't have the guts to deal with the sordid aspects of corporate life or because an impending lawsuit could follow if things go nastily awry. If so, they can pin everything on Larry, who keeps the "uppers" from taking the managerial hit. After all, it was Larry who pulled the trigger, not them. They're covered in the corporate scheme of things.

My second professional job found me on the other side of the aerospace aisle. I was selling hardware (titanium fasteners) to the manufacturing behemoth for which I had originally done purchasing. I believed I had found my true career destiny—the world of business-to-business corporate sales. When I was initially hired by this $100M firm, I had a great boss who also had a great boss. For the next four years, I received positive employee evaluations with subsequent raises in the form of both salary and bonuses. I felt I was an integral part of the team and a valued contributor.

Then during my fourth year, a large manufacturing firm from back east purchased the company. The new owner's business was mostly centered on automotive parts and accessories, but it had somehow found the aerospace industry to be alluring. So the company dropped a ton of dough and bought us.

The ripples from the takeover were fairly felt by all of us at the original company. My boss and his boss suddenly departed, and a new team was in the upper-middle echelon with all its members ready to make a name for themselves. A token sales guy was brought up from the salesman ranks to act as Sales Director until the company could hire the "right" individual to fill that slot. He was a good ol' boy from Texas who did not seem too harmful, but he didn't possess the first clue about how to run a sales team. He was a sales*man*, not a sales manager. Even so, he was a likeable cuss who didn't interfere with my world in the slightest. A company man of twenty years, he had no idea how he was being set up to fail.

His first assignment was to find "Larry." Larry was hired to take the role of sales manager while our unsuspecting Texan would "direct" activities in the yet-to-be-determined director position. Thus, when he arrived, Larry reported to the Lone Star State—no descriptor could have been better suited for him. And, of course, Larry was approved by the higher-ups. This decision was not made solely by our lone-acting Texan. As I said, the company was "insulating" since the announcement that Larry had been hired came directly from the newly appointed and soon-to-be-anointed, Director of Sales.

The first time I had the displeasure of meeting Larry face-to-face was at the corporate headquarters in his newly appointed office. Every paper on his desk was perfectly placed for easy access. A single pen, a phone, an inbox (with one paper on each shelf) sat next to the perfectly situated black leather desk pad. Three sales management books adorned the shelf to the left side of his desk (please note: none had ever been opened, let alone read; all were creaseless with no tears or blemishes). Everything was placed in exactly the right spot as if it had been carefully planned and executed by a Hollywood set designer. All the contents of his office fit in one box. Of course, he had the obligatory 5x7 framed desktop family photo of his non-descript smiling wife and his stroke-oaring, 4.0 student daughter.

Throughout our thirty-minute introductory conversation, not the hint of a smile cracked the corners of his thin-lipped mouth. In fact, the only action this man engaged in as we spoke was occasionally to move his pen from one side of his desk pad to the other, making sure it pointed in a perfect north-south direction. I watched as he adjusted it several times in order to align just so—with what, I wasn't quite sure.

The last thing we covered in our conversation was our expectations. He told me, "We expect you to increase sales by twenty-five percent this next year, and we will be giving you some legal forms to sign to ensure we are both in agreement on this." At this point, our conversation started to perk up a bit and suddenly headed in an entirely different direction. You see, my sole account, the very large aerospace giant, was in a downward cycle at this time (the mid-1980s) and everyone in the company/industry knew it. In fact, it was so well known that my company had been in negotiations for the previous two years to push the delivery of previously ordered products out until the production of the client's airplanes regained its earlier status. As I said, this fact was well-known and very common practice in the cyclical business of airplane construction. It was simply the way our industry ran during a down cycle, and we were in for an additional eighteen months more of the same. As soon as the airplane production line was increased, we'd start selling our product again. It was that straightforward. The original goal under previous management during such times was to maintain our position, find areas of opportunity, build our relationships, and be ready to pounce when the buying machine ramped up.

After I explained my situation, Larry presented a neatly organized, perfectly aligned stack of documents from his desk drawer on just exactly how the numbers broke down across product lines in my account. I looked them over, told him I thought it was all great, and I couldn't be more with him to make this happen. In my mind, though, I thought, *Why not double the amount?* I figured we had just as much chance of hitting that number as we did the lower one. After all, if we were stargazing, we might as well think big.

My next question for Larry was: "Given the new goals and the current business cycle we are in, how exactly do you see or plan for us to be successful in meeting these new targets?" His response was a classic Larryism; he looked me over and said, "That's not my problem. According to my predecessor, you're the *wunderkind* and as such, that's why we have you working on that issue. Your job is to make sales happen, and we expect a minimum 25% increase out of you, or we'll have to make the 'necessary adjustments.' After all, you're the voice of our company to the biggest account we have and it is projected that you will take us into the next decade and beyond."

I had no idea until then that I was so important!

When that meeting concluded, I was sent on my merry way back to the customer to start beating the dead and leafless bushes in my shrinking account so I could increase sales by twenty-five percent over the next twelve months or my company would have someone else to train. Imagine my glee.

For the next several months, my working life was a living hell. Nothing I did after that, or what I had done in the past, counted. In fact, what I had done previously was so seemingly horrible that I was summoned to Los Angeles for a "special" meeting with Larry and the Texan. In this meeting, I was cited for not meeting my objectives. Being unclear as to what these "objectives" exactly were at this juncture, I had to endure Larry promptly pulling out the identical stack of papers from his immaculately laid out desk—the same papers I had received in our initial meeting. The three of us then went page-by-page, item by excruciating item, through the stacks to locate each and every one of my shortcomings. After about four hours of grilling, I finally threw up my hands and said with a smile, "I surrender; you win. And seeing as how we've spent the past four hours going over my deficiencies, how about we spend the remainder of our time talking about my attributes?" Without a beat, Larry stated, "I wish I could, but I see none to identify." The Texan remained motionless and speechless, but I could see behind his pale eyes that he was along for the ride whether he wanted to be or not.

In that moment, I had been "Larryed." He was quick on the draw, and when I wasn't looking, he had got me with a clean shot right—right through my heart. As I sat across from those two after being pierced to my soul, I struggled to keep in my tears. Never in my working life had someone challenged my efforts and accomplishments to such a degree, merited or not.

But one thing that his comment did give me besides pain was closure. I got up, grabbed my bag, and announced, "I'm catching the next flight out of L.A. tonight. Whatever you decide to do, go for it; I'm just a phone call away."

Good ol' Lone Star stood up and said, "Hey, man, not so fast. Let's go have dinner. Why not spend the night before you head back?"

I thought to myself, *you must be on drugs after what we've just been through.* But I kept my composure and game face on and let on like it was water off a duck's back. "No, that's okay, but thanks for the offer. I obviously have a lot of work to do tomorrow so I need to get back." Of course, Larry was quick to pounce and tell Lone Star, "Sure, I'll go with you!" with his emotionless voice. I can only imagine the joy that dinner must have been between those two after that afternoon gathering… God bless them for "working" so hard into the night.

For the next couple of months, I plugged away and did everything possible to stay below Larry's radar. I knew I was one of his primary targets (did he really think the sales guys didn't talk to each other?).

Finally, the day came when Larry decided it was time to make the trek north and actually see what an airplane looked like while it was being assembled and where our products fit. I was dreading this day like none other to that point in my life, although I had decided before he arrived that my days with the company were numbered, and it was time for me to move on. I saw no future for me there, and the passion I had once had for my job had departed long ago.

I met Larry at the hotel that morning where we had breakfast together. As usual, he was his emotionless self with little to add to my outline for our day. I had set up meetings with all the key players: rivet supervisors, assembly foremen, engineers, and last, but not least, the purchasing department. All were lined up in perfect order so we could go from one interview to the next.

When we got out onto the assembly line, the rivet supervisor and I showed Larry exactly where our product was being used. First on our stop was the latest generation plane, which was still building about three planes per month. He saw the entire wing assembly that included over three thousand pieces (per wing) of our titanium fasteners. But instead of appearing pleased or impressed, he remained impassive, as if he were bored.

After we finished our tour with the customer, Larry calmly looked at me and said, "Now let's see all the places where we don't have our product installed." So off we went as I showed him just about every nook and cranny and rivet hole I knew in the plant. These were, for the most part, all on the old airplane, which we had only recently been approved to install. This was a small detail, mind you, but again, all Larry could see was that I had failed to sell more, and he couldn't wait to write that up in his report for headquarters.

Finally, all of our meetings with the customers ended and it was time to debrief. We made our way to a local watering hole where it got ugly fast. Larry proceeded to pull out my annual review, which was about as poor as it could possibly be, and he asked me to sign it. I refused and told him that if he really thought I was that poor of an employee, he should fire me. He said it was not that easy to fire someone these days. Then, without a pause he shot back, "Why don't you quit? It's clear you don't like it here." I proceeded to inform him that I was not a wealthy man and had not even considered leaving the company. Okay, so I wasn't quite truthful about the last part, but I wasn't about to let this asshole off without making him squirm like a worm on the end of a fishing pole.

From my perspective, at this point we were done. I got up,

looked him in the eye, and said, "I'll have the hostess hail you a cab so you can get back to your hotel." Then I turned and walked out. I wasn't about to spend the next thirty minutes or so in the same car with this heartless prick.

Following our last "collision," I decided it was time to let a few more people back at headquarters in on our little secret. I started writing letters to Human Resources throughout the organization all the way up to the parent company to provide the view of the world through my eyes. It elicited an immediate response. The HR director booked himself a flight to Seattle the day after he received it. But for me, it was already too late. I knew it, but I was now starting to have a bit of fun at this corporate dildo's expense by making his life as miserable as he'd made mine during the past several months.

When the HR director arrived, we met at his hotel and proceeded to go down the corporate HR track. I received an earful of "do this," "do that," "look at it this way," "work toward a winning scenario," etc., etc.—basically a load of HR psychological crap. When he finished, the HR director leaned forward and said, "The bottom line, Randy—you have to get along with your boss." I replied, "That will not happen in this or any other lifetime."

After receiving my Human Resources in a can, I made up my mind that I was finished. After the HR director left, I picked up the phone, called Lone Star, and resigned. The newly appointed Director politely accepted, said he was sorry (but didn't mean it), and that was that.

Although I had resigned, I was far from done and decided to lay a little napalm down on my way out of the jungle. Call it vindictive, because it was, and I can't say looking back now that I would take this route again, but at the time it sure felt good, and I was quite pleased with myself for what I was about to do.

All the key stakeholders (with regards to getting our products on the plane, the very ones whom Larry had met on his venture north, were not only my customers, but THEY HAD BECOME MY FRIENDS, something the geniuses back at Corporate failed to take into consideration before they acted as they did.

During my time at this job, I had joined several of my customers on numerous outings. Almost any event they had planned (skiing, hiking, soccer, dinners at their homes, golf games, attending professional sporting events, etc.), had included me. In fact, I even sent my customers and their wives flowers on their birthdays. In other words, we had become a tight group. I'm sure Larry had gone through my previous years' expense reports with a fine-toothed comb. Did he think my itemized bills were purely creative writing I had made up to pad my own wallet?

Hell, I had even gone hunting (even though I wasn't a hunter) with one of the "big" clients and shot a hole through his trailer while we were out in the woods (No, I hadn't mistaken his trailer for a deer). Even after that incident, my client still loved me. Of course, it made for some very funny banter in his office, "How on earth are you going to mount that over your fireplace?" but everyone was good-natured about my lack of hunting skills and expressed relief that at least I hadn't killed anyone.

Word was out and I made no effort to hide the fact that I'd been "Larryed." As a result, my customers heeded the call to action by removing many of the very fasteners I had worked so diligently to get installed on their airplanes during the previous five years. In the world of building airplanes, the manufacturer always has several vendor choices. Thus, my customers decided to exercise these options by replacing our product with brand "X" to send a message back to my former employer of how things worked in a good ol' boy environment.

About eight months later, my former customers told me that Larry had moved on to his next town. Then the dismissal of Lone Star came along with his boss, the General Manager. The ones who remained were the VP "cowboys" at the top who were responsible for the calamity in the first place. Funny how that works in corporate America—the elite remain the elite, no matter what happens in the lower echelons.

If you find yourself in a similar situation, just remember that you do have options. Dig in for the long haul and ride it out until the Spanish Inquisition has departed and maybe, just maybe, you'll someday regain your status. If your company is large enough, you might move to another department or branch to practice your trade. Or, you can move on to newer and more fertile ground. That's about it as far as your options are concerned.

Clearly if you're still early in your career with few obligations, it's easier to make this type of decision. For those in the middle of their careers or at a tipping point, the options will most likely appear more limited and less like options. People in mid-career or late career are the ones who really get stung in being "Larryed" because leaving your job may almost certainly be a career ender. Even so, consider your options—you may find a new career you will enjoy.

Looking back, I'm not proud that I took a vindictive course of action following my resignation. And if I come across as sounding like I was "victimized," then I have failed to make my point. The message here is that life is full of lessons for all of us, big and small, and I chalk this one up as a big one for me. I was twenty-seven at the time, and I trusted my gut that leaving was the right thing to do. My justification was that I was doing the company a favor by quitting so I didn't even negotiate a severance package, and since I was getting the short end of the stick, I stooped down to Larry's level. Looking back now, I see that was definitely a mistake.

Recently, I saw the film *Up in the Air* with George Clooney. He plays a contracted professional "Larry" who takes great pride in his work. In the end, he is alone, standing in front of an airline kiosk determining his next destination to fire yet another unsuspecting victim. When I watched this scene,

I couldn't help but recall "Larry" whom I suspect suffered a similar fate.

As for me, I learned what mattered most to me from that experience—my self-respect and integrity, and working in an environment where I was appreciated.

YOUR EXTRAORDINARY LIFE AND ITS WORTH

Sell It, Give It Away, or Own It

Before you get "Larryed," consider that in life, work, home, or play you have three choices: Give It Away, Sell It, or Own It.

You may choose to "Give It Away" by throwing to the wind decisions important to your future, your needs, or your desires. You cast a blind eye to your purpose allowing others to dictate what they think is best for you.

Or you may choose to "Sell It" to the highest bidder. You may be feeling disgruntled but instead of moving forward, you take solace in having "Sold It" for a reasonable price or conciliatory terms regarding emotional or financial gain. You are satisfied to settle into a routine of complaint as the victim, rather than "owning" the response and accepting the terms.

However, only one choice will lead to Living an Extraordinary Life and that is to "Own It." You "own" your life by choosing to see you are the one who is in control of it. You decide where you lay your hat, whom you keep as company, and how you respond to any given circumstance. You too can "Own It" if you choose to take responsibility for outcomes. You "Own It" by choosing your mindset, perspective, and your responses to the Larry's in the world. You are the "artist to your canvas."

Many of us are faced with working in an intolerable situation or working for supreme jerks. Chances are you will not get to leave the planet until you are faced with getting Larryed too. So...when in such a situation, remember you have three choices: Give It away, Sell It, or Own It. The choice is yours.

NO REGRETS

Life is too short to wake up with regrets.
Love the people who treat you right.
Forget about the ones who don't.
Believe everything happens for a reason.
If you get a second chance, grab it with both hands.
If it changes your life, let it.
Nobody said life would be easy.
God just promised it would be worth it.

Chapter 5

OWNING IT

DRIVE THY BUSINESS OR IT WILL DRIVE THEE.

— BEN FRANKLIN

Few things have been more rewarding in my life than running my own business. Founded in 1985, I called it Opal Enterprises after my recently deceased Grandmother, Opal (Getman). I am certain she is an angel among the divine, so I knew her name would give me an edge on whatever this world might throw my way in regards to the challenges of running a small business. After all, from where Grandma was sitting, she wouldn't possibly allow her namesake to be tarnished, wounded, or damaged. As one of my most astute revelations, I couldn't have been more spot-on with this belief.

Opal Enterprises started out by producing live theatre in the thespian district of Capitol Hill in Seattle. Literally building a theatre from the ground up in our teaching space, we hung a shingle and set out to produce a series of one-act plays. None of my business partners or coworkers had the foggiest idea what we were getting into or what we were doing other than knowing we wanted to act and make our living in the theatre. I figured the best way to accomplish this goal was to produce the type of theatre we liked.

The idea worked, and we made a small profit with every show we produced. Most theatre companies will tell you what we did is impossible; they resort to the world of the nonprofit 501C3 circles with their annual fundraising donation programs to stay in existence. The key for our model was maximizing our marketing spend to ensure it put paying cheeks in seats, negotiating the best deals possible on each and every expense, creating minimalist theatre and paying the actors/support staff based upon receipts, not steady salary. That way, everyone had a vested interest for making a show work from a financial standpoint. For the most part, the participants of such an arrangement were pleased because after all, they did not expect to get rich, just jointly to delve into the world they loved for the sake of art and to create the type of theatre they wanted to perform. It proved to be one of the greatest experiences of my life, and I can unequivocally say the same for those who partook in it.

TAKING YOUR NEXT STEP

Once I had the experience of acting, directing, and producing several local productions on the Seattle stage, I decided it was time to head to Los Angeles and try my hand in the big leagues of acting in film and television. That four-year experience would provide me with my "Master's Degree in Life." I packed my Peugeot four-door sedan and set out on a southerly course, soon to find out that what Frank Sinatra so wonderfully crooned in "New York, New York"—"If I can make it there, I'll make it anywhere" certainly pertained to Hollywood and its dog eat dog, no commitment, self-absorbed, and bedeviled world.

The only person I knew in Los Angeles at the time who worked in the "Industry" was Gordon Jump, the station manager character of "WKRP in Cincinnati" fame years before (he later became the Maytag repair man who sat around waiting for the phone to ring). I had met him in Seattle at an "Acting in TV" class where I had the great fortune to be seated next to his lovely wife Anna. Somehow, I made a lasting impression on her during the session since she gave me their phone number and invited me over to dinner at their house when I arrived in Los Angeles.

Gordon was represented by Abrams, Rubiloff and Lawrence commercial talent agency, and he got me an introduction with them. I was accepted and now had official agency representation (I'm certain because of his referral, not my on-camera abilities). This agency was a major player in the commercial talent world so I went on many auditions during my tenure with them. It took some time, but eventually I would get hired as a commercial actor for several national commercial spots. Commercials turned out to be a great learning experience for me about how to make a living while you sleep—I got paid a few hundred dollars every time one of my commercials aired.

I quickly acclimated myself to my new surroundings and got busy making contacts in any manner I could. I started my research with the overpriced trade rags and began calling production companies that were listing projects in the works. Early in my career during a commercial audition, I was standing in the waiting room with about fifty other guys of similar look and build. One of the hopefuls came up to me and said, "You look a lot like Jeff Daniels. Have you ever worked as his stunt double?" My answer was a resounding, "No" since I hadn't been in town long enough even to know it was a job option. He explained that he had stunted and stood-in for several actors. He said it was a great way to work, get "acquainted" with the process, and still get paid.

Low and behold, soon after while going through the trades, I saw notification of a new George Harrison film in the offing called "Checking Out," and the leading man—Jeff Daniels. It was going to be filmed entirely in Los Angeles, which was a huge benefit for a local actor who wanted to be the principal's stand-in/stunt double since a production company is unlikely to pop for out-of-town expenses for this position. I interviewed, got the job, and worked every day of a two-month production mirroring Mr. Daniels around the set since he was in every scene. As a result, I was paid a higher salary than half the crew and did a fraction of the physical work. All the while, I observed and learned the political hierarchy of a movie set and the inner workings of its exclusive environment.

One key protocol on the set was that I had to wait until the entire crew was served meals before I could be served because I was considered a second-class citizen on the set...I didn't care as long as I was being paid and still got fed. By the way, I also had the extreme privilege to meet George Harrison (the quiet Beatle), which made for an extraordinary experience.

THE POWER OF THREE

From this enterprise, I made several key contacts in the "Industry," which kept me working both in front of and behind the camera lens for the duration of my stay in Los Angeles. Soaps, commercials, casting directors, producers, agents, game shows, network television, industrials, pilots, other films and network promos, and product placement rounded out my partial list of leads. All came about as a result of the contacts I made on that first set. Another key learning experience I picked up at the time was the power of three—one introduction leads to three. I asked every person I met for three referrals. Before long, I had more people to contact than I had time in the day. Do the math and you'll know what I mean.

I made it my business to get hired by working my lists of one to three contacts exhaustively and methodically so I got introduced and indoctrinated into the world of film, both on the acting and the production side. Again, I felt if I approached things from the production point of view, I would have a significant advantage over the million plus people calling themselves actors in LA, who were running aimlessly from audition to audition between their real jobs.

An example of how my approach worked is when I was hired to be a reader for Ronnie Yeskel, a prominent casting director. I had auditioned for her while she was at LATC (a major downtown theatre company at the time). She told me she liked what she saw, so I contacted her relentlessly. I was finally hired to read several scenes for other actors auditioning for the director/producer of an episode of "LA Law." I ended up being hired as an actor in the show I was reading for the other actors. A small part, but it was work on a major show at the time. Imagine that—hired to perform support work with no promises, and ending up with a role on the show. By the way, I continue to receive twenty to thirty-cent residual checks for that episode since it's still running on a cable channel somewhere in the world! Another example (albeit small) of earn while you sleep.

Nine out of ten people I interviewed from the production side counseled me to become an agent. That's where the power and the real money lie. Over and over and over again I heard this battle cry. Agents were calling the shots in Hollywood by bundling actors, directors, writers, etc. under their command into productions for the studios. However, I didn't have the slightest desire to be an agent. I simply viewed it as keeping me from my goal of exploring my artistic side—acting—and it would have been a full-time job that would have done just that. I came to LA to act and produce, and by damn, that's what I was going to do. If I wanted a full-time job, I could go back to Seattle and live where the air was clean and be near my folks and closest friends. Nope, being an agent never entered my line of thinking.

KNOW WHEN TO REEVALUATE YOUR GOALS

I'm pleased to look back and know I stayed focused on my primary goal. When I went to Hollywood, it was to be a paid actor. In all that time, I never once waited tables, bartended, or performed any other "menial" job outside of the industry. I made my existence doing exactly what I went there to do— work in the "Industry." It was my dedication to that goal that made it reality.

After three years, however, as I grew to see Hollywood more and more from the inside for its real worth, my goals evolved into other areas and my desire to be a working actor diminished. It was time to move forward. I wanted to get married, have a family, and "settle" down. Leading the life of an actor/film production junky didn't figure into this scene. In my mind, it was too unstable, and Los Angeles was not a city where I wanted to raise kids. It was too transient, superficial, and crowded—not to mention exorbitantly expensive considering what you got in exchange in terms of bad air and water.

What followed next proved a challenging time in my life. I had given up all of my former professional identity to move to Los Angeles and pursue a goal I felt I had no option to avoid. It's amazing to me how strongly we can hold onto what was, and how we will allow our profession and finances to determine our view of ourselves. I was now the ripe old age of thirty-five—an age I believed to be over the hill...what on earth could I do? Who would hire an "old" guy to be in a real job? Was I finally destined to become a bartender? But what happened next was one of the most exciting and exhilarating rides of my life. I lost my way but I started a new career.

REJUVENATING YOUR ROOTS

When I returned to Seattle, I had no idea what I was going to do next. All I knew at that moment was to accept that I had lost my way and that an uncharted course lay before me. I was clueless about where it would lead. Nevertheless, I trusted my gut and my goal to settle down so I focused on making it a reality.

While I was in Los Angeles, a local Seattle-based company called Microsoft had gone "Big Time," and it had become the entire buzz in the local press. In my prior life as a salesman, I had sold hardware to the largest Aerospace manufacturer in the world, Boeing. It bought more hardware than any other company on earth, and since I had an affinity toward the aerospace industry at the time, I felt it would be as good a customer as any for selling my wares. After all, my dad had worked there for over thirty years, so Boeing was certainly a household name. Boeing employed the primary breadwinner of every other household on our block. The company was ubiquitous in the Seattle employment arena.

I had either consciously or subconsciously realized business to business sales was in my career bloodstream so targeting an organization with Boeing's buying power had a direct correlation to my thought process with Microsoft. It was big and getting bigger, and I was certain it needed to buy something I could provide. I just needed to find out what Microsoft was buying and marry it back to where my interests lay. I decided upon industrial film production and plied my trade in that area of expertise.

I use the term "industrial film production" loosely since I had virtually no idea what the hell I was doing when it came to producing videos for the likes of Microsoft in the early '90s. The company was on a tear, and I knew absolutely nothing about its business. What I did know, however, was how to make contacts and get myself in front of decision-makers whom I could then convince I would solve their problem—a strategy I had learned from my days in Los Angeles. I got in the door and the rest is financial history.

I had no idea how much money could be made selling to a company with bottomless pockets where everyone you dealt with needed whatever he needed yesterday. This production frenzy equated to insane budgets, crazy work schedules, and unstoppable excitement in a newly born industry trying to put a computer on every desktop worldwide. It was completely nuts and unbeknown in mankind's history with no roadmap in place. I hitched my wagon and got on for the ride of a lifetime.

For three years, I worked on some of the biggest launches of software products the Information Technology industry had to offer. The pace, schedule, and demands put on everyone involved to produce this work were amazing. It was truly a collaborative effort among vendors and staff, and I had the opportunity to work with some of the most dedicated, learn on the fly individuals you can imagine. Many of us pretended to know what we were doing, but if truth be known, most were in a "zone" of the imaginary. It was all too new, and the money being thrown around to make it come together was never before experienced. We just reacted because there was little opportunity to get ahead of it. It was all moving at the *speed of information*—a term Bill Gates later coined as the subject of his book.

FLEXIBILITY

In 1994, Microsoft decided it was time to "reorg" (reorganize) the entire company. This new term at the time would reflect a continual process that still occurs every few months to this very day. As with all maturing corporations, as new blood arrives, things change. The latest decision came from a bean counter in another part of the world that needed to make his mark. The result—Microsoft needed to let go of anyone and everyone who was not supporting its core business of producing software. As such, all who were fervently producing the marketing from an event tactical standpoint were let go and put on the street. These people were the ones who had hired my services, and now they were suddenly gone…literally in many cases, overnight. If I were to survive this calamity, it was time for me to reorg myself as well.

When major change occurs, you have two options. You accept it or you fight it. It's pretty amazing how many choose the latter course. Change is difficult and many people I've observed in my lifetime are adverse to it. Big time companies hold on to the bitter end to what they know, and they bury their heads in the sand to avoid the reality around them. I've experienced and learned firsthand in business over the years that if you are adverse or reject change, you're certain to die. Pure and simple, no questions asked. Harvard Business School is full of case studies on the subject, and there's little sense in mentioning the Blockbusters of the world. Just watch the way traditional newspapers will do business in the years to come. They will either have an electronic business model or they'll be out of business. The day of the printed page is rapidly declining because economics won't support the original distribution model. The only thing absolutely certain in life (besides death and taxes) is change.

So we at Opal Enterprises changed along with our client base. We decided to produce the very thing that Microsoft fired…event management. After all, the need hadn't gone away. Microsoft had just fired its entire staff that was performing this function. It didn't take a Wharton Business School major to figure this one out—no shortage of opportunity came about for our company from this major course adjustment in another's business management model.

With any business, once the market is established, competition sets in and it's inevitable you'll be challenged with the onslaught of competing services. It's part of the capitalistic system's beauty. I have always embraced and accepted it as it gives you the opportunity to prove yourself on merit, benefits, and features of your offerings above the competing factors. If you can't, you're dead the same as if you can't accept change. Embrace it and thrive, or avoid it and fail. It's a universal law and very clear-cut.

TAKE ADVANTAGE WHEN OPPORTUNITY COMES KNOCKING

Lower cost solutions inevitably appeared on the scene and our services were being commoditized. If I can stress anything in business to be aware of besides change and competition, it's being commoditized. And that's a tough one as just about everything in the world is commoditized these days. Just walk through any major retailer and see the options available for the same product. Costco, Sears, Best Buy, Lowe's, Home Depot, Macy's, Nordstrom, and Walmart at the brick and mortar stores (Internet resellers are even bigger) have endless displays of washers, dryers, flat screens, stereos, irons, shirts, pants, shoes, etc. from which to choose. How does one decide? Brand, price, color, style, shape, size, function, features, and benefits are good starters. There's hardly a business in existence today that isn't a commodity. Nevertheless, I preferred not to be commoditized, so Opal Enterprises sought out a differential that couldn't be shopped or bid against.

We found that differential via Corporate Sponsorship. The year was 1994, and for the most part, IT corporate sponsorship was in its infant stage. At least from the seat where I was sitting.

I had a good relationship with a very creative client on the marketing side, who wanted to do an entirely new and untried program. It needed to occur in eight U.S. cities simultaneously and be hosted by third party evangelists—non-Microsoft employee IT experts in their specific locale who "pretended" to be agnostic toward Microsoft. The fact is, they were spoon-fed the script and turned it into their own words on how best to use Microsoft Development Tools. It was a brilliant strategy for its time and grew to over 150 cities worldwide in less than two years.

The challenge this pilot program faced was my client had a total budget that would basically cover our execution fees, while he still had venue, launch, content, travel, marketing, video production, etc. to contend with—a number close to five times his total budget. He had the option to scrap it, scale back, do it entirely on the cheap, and/or hire less expensive vendors to execute the program. The latter was not something I wanted to see happen as it meant I wouldn't get the job.

Around this time, I had received a flyer from a Chicago-based organization named IEG. Its entire business model focused on the world of sponsorship—sports, corporate, naming rights, etc. If it could be sponsored, IEG covered it. The company had an annual seminar around this time so I figured it was worth the two or three thousand dollars investment to attend. My assumption proved correct as I walked out of the weeklong conference with a new business model that would solve my clients' problem—corporate sponsorship. I was fired up.

What I learned that week was the power of leverage and what sponsorship was about. Microsoft being the powerhouse that it was in the developer space, it was certain if you promoted an event to a particular target audience on the virtues of using Microsoft tools, the customers would come. And guess what, these same customers also need hardware to run, places to buy the software, magazines to read about it, and accompanying tools to make it all work. Thus, the very same Microsoft model of using partners to help sell wares, which is even greater today than it was fifteen years ago.

On the plane home from Chicago, I pounded out a rough draft of a proposal outlining the benefits of incorporating sponsors so we could fund the entire eight-city event and still have money left over as a contingency. Opal's sponsorship fee was based entirely upon the success of our ability to sell sponsorships.

Nothing was really novel here—just a basic commission-based sale with Opal acting as the Microsoft broker to its target partner audience. After all, Microsoft needed to remain agnostic to its partner community and not show any favoritism. There were dozens of hardware Original Equipment Manufacturers (OEM's), hundreds of Independent Software Vendors (ISV's), resellers, service providers, publications, etc. But only ONE Microsoft—the glue that held all of these partners together.

I sat down with my client one-on-one, presented the

proposal, walked him through it step-by-step and showed him exactly how the program would make him a success to his management. Opal Enterprises got the job, and it turned out exactly how it was planned. From a handful of Microsoft Partners, we raised over half-a-million dollars for that prototype marketing program. The result—client happy, Microsoft Partners happy, Microsoft customers happy, Opal Enterprises happy. We had stumbled upon a perfect model at the time for a "Win, Win, Win, Win" scenario. Not only had we covered our event management fees, but we were paid a percentage of the gross sponsorship sales (thus increasing our bottom-line and creating a completely new service offering).

Most importantly, we had a surefire model now to keep us employed, no matter what the budget constraints might be, and to keep the competition completely out of the equation. We were offering something no one else offered, and thus, it could not be commoditized. But the best was yet to come.

Microsoft's Developer Relations Group (DRG) was responsible for several of the company's largest customer outreach events. While most events fell under DRG jurisdiction, an independent owner ran each event with little to no crossover between events. From its inception, Microsoft has run this fragmented business model. As it has grown and progressed, Microsoft executives have tried numerous times to create an overarching business model in certain marketing areas, but the model still eludes them since the company is just not built that way. It remains broken up by a lot of different internal businesses that have their own profit and loss objectives. As such, the senior managers all the way down to the administrative assistants are graded based upon a scale of accomplishment. If something gets in the way from a competing internal group, it gets run over because the individuals will do whatever necessary to meet their individual objectives. No one is willing to take an individual hit to the chin for the overall organization's betterment. It's just the way the company is built, and Microsoft's success makes it difficult to argue with how it runs its business.

By working as an umbrella entity, the overreaching outside vendor can save the day for these various independent events. Opal came in and created an overreaching partner integration program that was consistent from one program to the next with measured results. It was beautiful! Over the next ten years, my company was responsible for raising over One Hundred Fifty Million Dollars in partner funds to assist Microsoft in producing its events. And that, my dears, is a perfect case study of the power of leverage and discovering an opportunity based upon talking and reacting to a client's pain point.

FIND YOUR NICHE

In 1998, I had the good fortune to be invited to attend a Microsoft partner meeting in Seattle with several top executives presenting the future as it would relate to the partners in attendance. My invitation was predicated upon my selling future sponsorships to these companies, so I was in the position to field questions and discuss opportunities.

Following one of the keynote presenters, the arena was opened up for questioning. I was seated in the second row, a perfect perch from which to observe the masses make up their inquiries. One of the first questions was from a local service provider with whom I had done some Microsoft related business in the past. He took the time to compliment the presenter on a great presentation and outline of the future opportunities available from partnering with Microsoft. He went on to say that Microsoft had done an amazing job of reaching the developer audience over the years and getting it to build to the Windows platform. However, his target customer audience was the business decision-makers or "C" level customers (CEO, CIO, CFO, CMO, CXO). Immediately, the congregation chimed in. The din from its inquisition was staggering as everyone stated a similar challenge. The presenter backed up and deferred to another colleague who conveniently happened not to be in the room at the time.

Wow, in that very moment an entire market of opportunity I had been overlooking just presented itself before my eyes. The audience of the Business Decision-Maker (BDM) was about to unfold and become a major factor in Opal's business mix. After all, if the companies that wanted to reach this particular customer sect were willing to pay for it, we needed to figure out a way to get to them. The answer became a sister company to Opal Enterprises—CXO Golf.

CXO Golf's name says it all, but for those unfamiliar with the vernacular, allow me to clarify. As I mentioned, in our business circle, the term "C" level customer denoted executive "X" officers and "O" level decision-makers, thus "CXO." Golf was the means to reach and engage them.

The first major golf tournament that CXO Golf produced for Microsoft was attached to its World Wide Partner Group, which had started an annual event in 1996 called Fusion. The conference's objective was to invite the major (and not so major) Microsoft Partners to a weeklong event for IT business education (and networking). Armed with the information I had garnered from the earlier presentation, I approached the group's General Manager (GM) in 1999 and presented to him my findings and proposal. Before I had a chance to get into the nitty-gritty, however, he cut me short, and in his most effective English accent, said, "Randy, Randy, Randy, Partners don't want to play golf; Partners want Content! Partners come to Microsoft to hear what we're doing and where the business opportunities lie." I didn't disagree, but all of my research showed that the partners wanted to hear the thirty thousand foot level keynote and network, and not necessarily in that order.

I began to show him my background research and statistics on the subject, how organized networking was a must, the merits of golf to accomplish such goals, the correlation to business, and the overreaching theme of business partnership being garnered during a round of an organized golf event. I had done my homework, and I felt it was a sure-fire presentation proposal with the outcome being a slam-dunk. But I couldn't have been more wrong. He would have no part of it because he was absolutely convinced it was folly and had no place at his Microsoft Partner conference. I left the meeting without a deal and only my detailed researched proposal in hand.

Throughout that year, CXO Golf got the business underway and produced several golf events for other companies and organizations. None, however, were on the scale of what we had proposed for the World Wide Partner Conference. With this experience and tried and true information in hand, I had the testimonial aspect and revamped the proposal for the next year's event.

That year, we also had something that was inherent with Microsoft—a new owner at the top. When I approached the newly appointed official with my amended proposal, low and behold, he bit. We were off to the CXO Golf races with regards to an event model that utilized golf with Microsoft Partners as sponsors, and was attached to a worldwide conference with several thousand attendees. Again, no trail blazing here, but it was completely new to Microsoft, the largest software company in the world with thousands of partners to target.

The model worked well, and everyone on all sides of the green was thrilled. With every project we produced, we made it a habit proactively to garner customer evaluations. With this project, we took extra care due to its magnitude and importance to prove the model and our point. The scale was 1 to 5 for the metric with the event garnering a 4.85 overall. This level was unprecedented for our organization (and most other programs of similar caliber). We all walked away pleased to know we had a winner.

Most importantly though, the golf event was the buzz of the conference, and all the participants lucky enough to participate took it upon themselves to tell anyone and everyone that golf was exactly what had been missing in past years, and how great it was of Microsoft to put something of this quality together for the purpose of structured networking.

I had observed an opportunity based upon customer input, dreamed up a solution which mapped to my company's interests and skill set, made a plan of attack, and executed it with a "win, win, win" business arrangement. The outcome meant we were paid well and taken to a new level where we had a surefire annuity-generating business model that served us well for several years.

I loved running Opal Enterprises and building it from the ground up to become a multi-million dollar operation. The company remained profitable for over forty consecutive quarters before I sold it—a feat we were all extremely pleased with since the market was extremely volatile (as it usually is) during many of those quarters. As a business, Opal Enterprises had all around been a "win-win" for its owner, employees, and customers.

MASTERY POINTS TO LEARN ON YOUR BUSINESS JOURNEY

In this chapter, I have gone into extensive detail about how the journey of owning one's business can unfold. I hope and trust the message of change rings loud and clear and you now understand the necessity of listening to your customers' needs. It is not my intention to chronicle *my* path or bring light to my accomplishments or losses. My purpose is to present basic steps I learned through my education in the business world that you can relate to your own situation and thereby make your journey as a more enlightened individual.

Here in a nutshell are the key points I presented here:

- Be passionate about what matters most in life to you.

- Follow your heart.

- Trust your instincts.

- Take advantage of it when opportunity knocks.

- Understand that while luck plays a role, it's what you do with it when it presents itself that matters.

- Know when to reevaluate your goals.

- Be flexible.

- Find your niche.

- Money does not equate with happiness.

- Networking is essential (it's who you know and how you know them that matters).

- It's okay to lose your way—you never know what opportunity may present itself when you're lost.

- Change is the only sure thing in life.

- Handling adversity is a must for success.

- Balance is key.

- Have faith.

- Find your philosophy.

- You can lose your car, house, and belongings, but no one can take away your experiences.

- Earn while you sleep.

- Make your clients successful.

- And last but certainly not least, customers will tell you exactly where the opportunities lie.

Despite all Opal Enterprises' success, the business took a toll on my person and my life. It was a high price to pay, so the thrust of the rest of this book will shed light on how to co-mingle a business life with a personal life to keep the former from consuming you so you don't lose sight of what is truly important. Businesses will come and go, but your family, friends, and health are non-negotiable when it comes to living an Extraordinary Life.

Living your life as if you have cancer will help you keep things in perspective.

Chapter 6

BECOMING
COLT HODGES

Hollywood is an extraordinary kind
of temporary place.
— John Schlesinger

The entire Los Angeles/Hollywood voyage was one of the more interesting times in my life. I always refer to it as "a break in my journey" because it felt like going away to college. I thought I was receiving my "Master's Degree in Life" by going to do something completely new in a faraway land. It was chock-full of real life survival experiences from the moment I arrived until the day I departed, and it remains one of the best learning lessons I ever received.

Going to Hollywood in the manner I did broke life down into a case of sheer survival. My life became a chapter right out of Maslow's hierarchy of needs, with focus on food and shelter, then love, self-esteem, and finally self-actualization. When I arrived, I had no means to make money and no shelter from the storm. It was fundamental survival at its civilized finest.

I also had neither love nor self-actualization. About the only thing I had underneath my feet was self-esteem, and even that was on shaky ground. A man without a country or a roof can find his foundation shaken pretty fast. But I had a dream and a goal that provided enough footing from which to begin.

Fortunately, I at least had food and water covered. Housing was another story since I didn't have a solid lead on solving this basic need. I had been working with a rental agency before I arrived to find an apartment, but I had only rolled snake eyes so far. It was next to impossible to know what you would get without visiting the place since there was no Internet at the time, only a description of the property with price, location, number of rooms, pets or no pets, parking, etc. Ultimately, I resorted to the newspaper's listings upon my arrival.

I love Los Angeles. I love Hollywood. They're beautiful.
Everybody's plastic, but I love plastic. I want to be plastic.
— **Andy Warhol**

Los Angeles is mostly made up of characters. If you want to meet some of their finest, pull out the shared housing list from the *Los Angeles Times* and start making calls. After screening several outbound inquiries and narrowing my list of drive up's, it was time to hit the pavement. My first stop was a guy who had what sounded like a pretty cool place tucked away in the Hollywood Hills. His name was Diego, which made a thousand images I should have paid closer attention to come to mind. When I knocked on the door of what appeared from the outside to be a decent home in an area I liked, my mind was open, but the second the door released from the latch, my mind closed. Before me stood a guy about five foot eight, conditioned, tanned, and for the most part, naked. He wore a loincloth I'm positive he found hanging on the staircase rail and strapped around himself on his way to the door. Complete with long dark hair, my immediate thought was that he was trying out for the next Tarzan movie. "Good," I thought, "because if he gets it, I'm a shoe-in to read for the part of Cheetah."

Diego and I introduced ourselves. Since I had made the trek up the hill, I figured, "What the heck; let's hear what this guy has to offer." First I asked him his family name to go along with his Christian one. Low and behold, he had none. He was only called "Diego" (which I'm certain was fictitious). Following this response, I decided to leave all questioning on the table and just listen from there on out. He was in the "arts" and paraded around the house light-footed much like a ballet dancer while making strong emotional gestures to draw my attention to particular subjects—mostly paintings or statues of naked men and women.

When I had seen all I needed to see (no pun intended), he asked how I felt about "nudity." I told him I had no real issues with it in its proper time and place, but it wasn't something I gave a lot of thought to on a daily basis. He replied, "Well, I like to be nude and so do most of my friends, so if you have difficulty with nudity, there most definitely would be a 'problem'." At this point, I was doing my best to keep a straight face since I had clearly stumbled upon a masterpiece L.A. character. I reiterated that nudity was not a big issue for me, but not since high school PE had I been around a lot of naked men all in one place. He explained that he wasn't "gay" and the women who came over often quickly became clothes-free as well. As good as that might sound, I guess I was having some visual issues (especially if I wanted to have a date over). After I told him it probably wasn't the ideal living situation for me, we shook hands, thanked each other for his time, and I went off to my next housing adventure. I was grateful that "Diego" had at least kept his loincloth on during my visit.

Meeting Andrea was another memorable housing moment, again in the hills of Hollywood. On the phone, she told me the house was having some renovation work done which was scheduled to be finished in the near future, and that the room for rent had a fabulous view. The price was right and I was intrigued enough once again to drive up into the hills. When I arrived, lumber was strewn across the hillside, and much of it was now part of the undergrowth. I could only surmise that the renovation had been going on for some time.

Andrea was a comely woman in her early forties. From the looks and smell of things, she liked to smoke pot and would have been more in her element living in San Francisco's Haight district than in the hills of Los Angeles. Pot smoking paraphernalia adorned the dwelling as did the smell of sandalwood incense. The only thing missing was the scent of patchouli oil.

On the inside, the house was upside down and a complete wreck. She apologized for the appearance and said she hadn't had time to straighten-up before I arrived because she'd been busy organizing her "thoughts." From the looks of her lifestyle, I'm sure thought-organization was a fulltime job that started at dawn (or whenever she arose) and went long into the wee hours of the night. As she gave me the tour, I felt amused even though I knew I was no closer to solving my housing dilemma.

When we reached the room for rent, I looked up to discover a good part of the room had no roof. It had been demolished "some time" before, and eucalyptus leaves from the trees above covered the floor. When I asked Andrea about the "hole" in the ceiling, she quickly replied that the repair would be completed "soon." If I agreed to move in and pay up front, it would happen even more quickly. After I politely refused the room, it was time for me to move on. I didn't even get high.

Driving back down the hill, I realized the room hadn't even had the promised view. Then it dawned on me—the "view" she had stressed was not of the city, but of the stars at night. From that experience, I learned to get more specific with my questioning. My image of living in the hills of Hollywood in a guesthouse with a rich starlet in the main house was quickly fading into the Los Angeles sunset.

Finally, perseverance paid off, and I found an apartment to share with a wonderful English woman about my age. One more tier on the survival pyramid solved. I moved in, and we remain friends to this very day.

Once the housing situation was resolved, onto the next level…making a living. Or was that finding love? As far as I was concerned, I put them both in the same category since members of the opposite sex were prolific, and I quickly found that work was available if you put forth the time to find it. I put it all to work in a diligent and structured way, and soon I was working in one capacity or another in the "industry." Since every job had a surplus of the opposite sex, it wasn't too terribly hard to kill two birds with one stone.

My goal was to be an actor, so I listened to everyone I ran

into for tips on the best way to be hired by someone capable of making that happen. I enrolled in scene acting classes, improvisation, acting for the screen, commercial acting secrets, buying script scenes, plays, etc. There was virtually no end of shenanigans and shysters to take your money in order to make you a star. Each one represented him or herself emphatically as the where all/end all to make you the next Robert De Niro or Al Pacino. For the most part, these classes made no difference in my getting hired for what I came to Hollywood to do. Mind you, it was always good to practice and work on my "craft." But in the Hollywood world of acting, having "talent" was about four or five rungs down the ladder from what was actually required. I viewed this as a plus, mind you, since I was not a very good actor.

Everyone said that if you want to be a real actor, go to New York.
If you want to sell out, go to LA. And I thought—
I want to sell out!
— **Jennifer Tilly**

Making a "living" my first year was comprised of me getting a few commercials and working production jobs in a variety of capacities, including being stunt double to Jeff Daniels. Almost every job I got was the result of networking, not being a talented or capable actor. The classes I so diligently attended were for the most part a complete waste of time, energy, and of course, money. I would have been far better served taking those assets and investing in my own projects as I had done in Seattle before heading south. Something happened in the change of latitude though that prevented me from keeping my bearing on what worked and what didn't. Being in Los Angeles negatively impacted my psyche by making me feel inferior compared to how capable I felt elsewhere. I never did figure out why this was the case, but at the root was a fear-induced feeling that I just wasn't good enough or in "their" league. What a joke it is now to contemplate that misguided belief.

One of the classes for getting hired as a commercial actor did eventually pay off. The instructor told our class we needed to have a good clean joke handy that was a real life story we could tell succinctly with the utmost clarity and timed delivery. In other words, make it personal, short, and sweet. Here's what I came up with:

> I have a friend with a farm in the nearby town of Carnation. On it he has a Sow. One night he and his wife were driving home and noticed the neighbor had put a sign up at the gate stating, "Pig for stud." They got to thinking about it and thought it wouldn't be such a bad idea to have a few piglets rooting around the place.

> The next morning he called his neighbor and said he would bring his pig over for the big event. So he went out and put her in the wheelbarrow and carted her across the field and dropped her off. "Come back about 5:00 p.m. to pick her up," spouted the neighbor.

> When the man came back he asked, "How do I know if it took or not?" "Tomorrow morning if she's eating grass, that means it took, and if she's eating hay, that means it didn't," was the reply.

> Next morning, the farmer goes out and sees the little darling munching away at the hay. So he puts her back in

the wheelbarrow and heads east across the field. Same reply ensues. Back at 5:00, grass or hay the next morning.

Well, this goes on for over a week. On the morning of the tenth day, the farmer is sitting at the kitchen table drinking his coffee when he says to his wife, "What's that pig doing, eating grass or hay?" His wife peers out through the window and replies, "I hate to say it but she's doing neither." "She's doing neither; so what the hell is she doing?" snapped the farmer. "She's sitting in the wheelbarrow," replied the wife.

About a dozen commercial auditions later, I was standing in front of the video camera and before the producer, director, casting director, agency personnel, and an assortment of non-essential support staff. When I walked into the room, the director called me out by name and stated they were shooting a commercial for a major global bank and wanted to depict an Irish wedding. Being of English heritage, I thought sure, no problem, smiled a great big Hollywood "I need this job in the worst way" smile, and said, "I'm your groom, best man, bride, or ring bearer; take your pick." He laughed and said, this was a non-speaking commercial (these by the way comprise about ninety percent of commercials), and all they were seeking was the right mix of wedding attendees with the "correct" look. Then he asked me to tell him a joke.

The next day I received a call from my agent stating I got the part, and I needed to show up at such and such a studio on such and such a date, and I would be hearing directly from the production team on specifics. That pig joke put more than fifty thousand dollars in my pocket because the commercial not only ran and ran and ran on national television, but it also was put into the bank's annual report, print ads, and a myriad of other sidebar paying aspects of being hired, and all because I made that guy laugh. I never lost sight of having a good, clean joke handy following that audition.

Growing up with the name Randy Broad certainly presented some challenges, especially during the junior high school years. It's a good thing I wasn't a boxer because I would have definitely received and given out some broken noses. I let my tongue do my fighting, and I won more than I lost. Yes, having the surname of "Broad" has some character building attributes attached to it, so I am not the least bit remorseful.

The first time I went to London, I introduced myself to a triage of women, "Hi, I'm Randy Broad. What are you up to tonight?" They immediately blushed, then laughed and jeered at the Yank before them. They departed and I was left wondering what on earth I had said that was so incredibly hysterical. A day later, I learned the direct translation of what I had said was, "Hi, I'm 'Horny Woman.' What are you up to tonight?" Case closed. For the rest of trip, I was known as "Hank."

Back to Hollywood—or rather Utah, where I was working on *"Ski Patrol"* which was based on the film *Police Academy*. I made friends right off with the production's still photographer who was as Kiwi as they come. He was a true New Zealander through and through with David Niven good looks. When I introduced myself to him as "Randy Broad," he nearly busted a gut and buckled over with laughter. Mind you, he was about half my size in height and weight, but he was still overcome by my introduction. He said, "Dude, if you ever go to New

Zealand, you're either going to get fucked or killed; there will not be anything in between." He went on to say, "Are your parents comedians? Because if they are, that's the funniest joke I've ever heard. I've never heard a name like that in my life." He continued to howl.

Let's rewind here to a trip to Palm Springs a few weeks before I headed off to Utah. I was sitting in the bar of the newly opened Ritz-Carlton and just so happened to be seated next to an elderly gentleman who liked his scotch. His name was Bob, and we connected immediately. We made our introductions and launched immediately into each other's background. He was in an estranged marriage with one of the past head producers of the popular soap opera "General Hospital." She had not only been responsible for getting Elizabeth Taylor on the show but also for creating the entire "Luke and Laura" hysteria around daytime television, which was so HUGE she made a gazillion dollars because of this mid-day renaissance. Her husband, Bob, was along for the ride (and the bottle of scotch), but he knew his stuff and specifically how the game was played. After we threw back a couple of more scotches, he showed me a few of his cards. He was blurry-eyed but his resonance was clear. He looked me straight in the eye, leaned forward, bobbed his head a bit and said, "I like you, and I think you have a future in this business. I've noticed you've caught the waitress' attention. But you have to do something about that name. 'Randy Broad' just isn't going to work; you need to come up with something better."

I was in it at that moment for the next drink and didn't give his advice a lot of thought. But he persisted and gave me his number to call him when I got back to Los Angeles. He told me he'd do whatever he could to help, even though he was on the outs (due to his drinking challenges) with his "General Hospital" success-filled wife. He said he still knew a few people and wanted to be a resource to accelerate my career. When he also stated he was a member of the Belair Golf and Country Club, I made no bones about it being the perfect venue for continuing our discussion. We met up a few weeks later to play a round of golf with a plastic surgeon formerly married to Eva Gabor. Just in time for me to try out my newfound identity.

Between the desert and the golf outing, I had been in contact with my friend John back home. He was telling me that he and Karl (a mutual friend) had gotten together and decided I needed a Hollywood name to make the big time. "Colt Hodges" was their brainchild. At first I laughed, but considering the recent advice, my hearing was more acute than in the past, so I told John I would think about it. That afternoon, I was sitting in my apartment watching black and white reruns of the 1960s television show "Rawhide." I remembered enjoying the show as a kid, but I had never paid too close attention to its characters. The one thing I did remember was Clint Eastwood got his Hollywood start on this show as the perennial wrangler, Rowdy Yates. Since I had a great-uncle named "Rowdy," I thought for a brief moment that might be the way to go. Just then the trail boss "Gil Favor" appeared on the screen. In this particular episode, he carried a "Colt Forty Four" revolver and with his first name being 'Gil', reminded me of Gil Hodges of Brooklyn / LA Dodger fame. Those were too many coincidences for me to pass up. "Colt Hodges" I became. Bob loved it, and he recited how Cary Grant, John Wayne, and a host of other major Hollywood stars' names had been changed to help launch their careers.

From then on, to every casting director I met, I introduced myself as "Colt." I changed the name on my photos, resume, and acting-related letters. As far as production work went, I kept Randy Broad and Opal Enterprises. But for everything else, I was Colt Hodges, and I took on a new persona. When about nine or ten auditions for the next commercial took place, guess what—I got hired. This time it was for Michelob Beer— two separate commercials that ran and ran across the sports filled screen, mostly during the Masters and US Open Golf Tournament because the commercials were of a golfer who on both occasions couldn't quite get the ball to drop in the hole. I can't help but think about the irony of life and the sequence of how things work out. Go ahead and call me crazy, spiritual, or whatever, but somehow, I don't feel any of this was brought about by coincidence.

The Los Angeles expedition moved forward for a few more years, and I continued to move up Maslow's needs list. Food, water, love, and self-esteem had been covered in abundance. And becoming Colt Hodges finalized the pinnacle of the pyramid— self-actualization. One of the greatest pieces of the Colt Hodges era was the creation of another identity while staying who I was and staying true to myself. I liken it to Darwin's theory of survival. Look in the wild at the bugs, animals, reptiles, and humans who have mimicked their surroundings and "evolved" over time to live in and adapt to their local environment in order to survive. We've all seen the bugs that look like the branch of a tree, white rabbits in a snowstorm, and deer coats that resemble the fauna of the forest floor. No difference exists here in my view from becoming or evolving into something in order not only to survive but to thrive in the environment you inhabit. Had I stayed in the aerospace business, perhaps I would have evolved into "Bolt McHenry" or some such pseudonym and become a fastener salesperson extraordinaire, the likes of which the world had never seen. Who knows? The fact is that I needed to be "Colt Hodges," play that part, and fit into my surroundings while remaining who I ultimately was—Randy Broad.

Colt Hodges has become a distant memory, but it's one I hold very near and dear to my heart. During that time, I grew exponentially as I was forced to survive in a world I knew little about. It was one adventure after another and made for an extraordinary time. I cannot recommend enough for you to step forward and discover your "Colt Hodges" as you live life as if you have cancer.

YOUR INNER SUPERHERO

Mastering Your Extraordinary Life

If you don't have cancer you might say, "I am afraid to live an Extraordinary Life." If you have cancer you might say, "I'm afraid not to live." The actor Christopher Reeves of Superman fame, after being tragically paralyzed in a horseback riding accident, said, "The most difficult thing about being paralyzed is watching able-bodied people walk through their lives as if paralyzed."

Christopher Reeves was right. Why are we moving through our lives as if paralyzed?

Extraordinary Lives are created by ordinary people like you— people who are willing to risk and to believe in themselves to move forward in their lives. Regular individuals who are ready to own their "Inner Superhero" wrestle their personal paralysis and get out of their own way to impact the world, regardless of the crazy fear that goes on in their heads. All the while, they remain mindful that as they reach toward their dreams, they must not sacrifice what is most important to them.

Our capacity is powerful beyond what we often recognize, but in our reckoning, we still must take action and move through paralysis to capture our potential. We must stand up and throw our imaginary superhero capes on and answer our personal callings.

We may be a bit bruised, but we won't be broken from the journey. Instead, we will emerge with a stronger sense of self and our own "Master's Degree in Life." We forge ahead in our perfectly imperfect state with fortitude, grace, and balance, which is well worth the risk of never having gotten off our tails to live an Extraordinary Life. So if you are currently sitting with fear, get off your duff and grab your cape…the world is waiting for you.

MASTERY QUESTIONS

What limiting beliefs do you have about yourself?

_____

_____

How do these beliefs sabotage your ability to live your Extraordinary Life?

_____

_____

Write down actions you will take to move you closer toward what you consider to be an Extraordinary Life.

_____

_____

Our deepest fear is not that we are inadequate.
Our deepest fear is that we are powerful beyond measure.
It is our light, not our darkness that most frightens us.
We ask ourselves, who am I to be brilliant, gorgeous,
talented, and fabulous?
Actually, who are you not to be?
— **Marianne Williamson**

Chapter 7

MISSING IT

CARPE DIEM! REJOICE WHILE YOU ARE ALIVE; ENJOY THE
DAY; LIVE LIFE TO THE FULLEST; MAKE THE MOST OF
WHAT YOU HAVE. IT IS LATER THAN YOU THINK.
— HORACE

If you live in the contiguous forty-eight, you know few things
are as exciting as freshly fallen snow. I remember as a four year
old making my way downstairs from our North Seattle home
to fetch Dad the morning paper. Upon opening the door that
early December day, I was surprised by the precious little tufts
of white floating down to their final destination.

I immediately bolted back upstairs, tore into my sleeping
sister's room, and screamed at the top of my lungs that it was
"SNOWING!" She, being tired of my pranks, decided I was
calling wolf, rolled over, pulled her pillow over her head, and
snarled, "Go away; you're annoying." In my glee, I continued
trying to motivate her to rise, get dressed, and come see for
herself. She continued to protest, concluding, "There's no way

it's snowing. It's way too warm, and it wasn't snowing last night when we went to bed." I enthusiastically replied, "Well, then I'm not sure exactly what it's doing, but it's falling from the sky and there's lots of it…and it's white!" She finally got up.

Perhaps I'm presumptuous in stating the entire lower forty-eight feels the excitement of snow since those in Buffalo, Minneapolis, Cleveland, or Denver, may not share my enthusiasm. That said, if you live in Seattle, snow is a BIG deal. If you're skeptical, just turn on the local news—even the remote prospect of snow on the horizon would make you think Jesus himself had sent a press release on his eminent arrival.

When the fallen snow reaches a depth of one inch (or less), you can count on Jim Forman of KING 5 News to be perched at the base of Queen Anne Hill donned in parka, stocking cap, and gloves, sensationalizing the event with his chirping quips, "The best advice is, IF you don't have to go out…DON'T… Live from lower Queen Anne, I'm Jim Forman KING 5 News." It's a joke, but it does get viewers to watch and thus sells advertising.

When my kids, Riley and Emily, were seven and eight respectively, we received one of those wonderful winter storms. The conditions were perfect the night before, and one could see the dull gray sheet of cloud cover roll in from the west. Anyone with a Seattle heritage knew exactly what was in store. The temperatures were sub-freezing and not remotely affected by the warmth the cloud cover often presents. With the impending storm, the air filled with the excitement only kids can create at the prospect of playing in the snow while school is cancelled.

That night, I emailed my employees to inform them not

to attempt to make their way to the office. Seattle comes to a complete standstill with even the slightest amount of white on its roads. With our laptops, we could function without physically being in our offices.

The next morning, we awoke to a blanket of pure delight— four to five inches of untracked velvety white scenery. The kids wolfed down their breakfasts while their mother struggled to pull coats, boots, hats, and gloves over their excitement. The sense of urgency filled the room and expanded to every corner. Boom—they were out the door with shouts of joy and sleds in hand.

We were fortunate to live on a dead-end street with a short yet steep hill. It was the perfect run for kids their age since they didn't have to walk too far or long and could still experience an amazingly fast ride. But it was steep, so even at a young age, a dozen treks in five inches of snow uphill with sled in tow was a meaningful workout.

My wife summoned me out the door that morning to share the experience of all that was good; family, snow, kids, dogs, and the joy it all brings. Still in my pajamas, I stated I'd be "right" out—I needed to check email first to make sure nothing was on fire.

I found my way into my home office and proceeded to respond to several dozen emails that materialized over night. About an hour into it, my wife appeared in the door with snow, sweat, and a smile, to ask, "Are you coming? The kids are having a ball. You're missing a great time." I told her again I'd be "right out" and sunk my head into my screen to continue my email responses.

More time transpired, and once again, my wife popped her snow-clad self in the door. This time, she was a bit more agitated and imploring that I needed to get out from behind my computer, get dressed, and get outside. Some more time transpired before I found my way to sifting through the closet of snow clothes.

I appeared on the scene to find exhausted, wet, soaked kids with red rosy cheeks. They were done and the snow that had been so pristine had taken on a different sheen. Rain had begun and the freshness of the early morning had melted into the afternoon.

As the kids made their way to the house to warm themselves with cocoa, my wife looked over her shoulder at me and quietly said, "You missed it." I stood there by myself with the kids' sleds in hand while rain dripped off the end of my nose.

It brings me great sadness on many fronts to recount this moment. To chronicle it for posterity's sake only serves to deepen the crevasse I feel in my heart. I champion myself as someone who spends little time contemplating the past because it's just a huge waste of energy when there's nothing you can do to change it. Regrets, I have few. Yet this memory haunts me more than I care to admit. I recall telling myself, "We'll do it later; it'll happen then." Unfortunately, the next year the kids were older and it didn't snow. I had missed it.

If you were to offer me a million dollars to recant what was so important to spend the morning sitting in front of my computer in lieu of sledding with my kids, I'd come up empty. Blank. I can't remember the contents of a single one of those emails. Yet I can recount the sights, smells, and excitement of that snowy day with such clarity it could have happened today. What does that say? Sitting in your home office pounding out meaningless emails, or sledding with your kids during a once in a lifetime moment—which matters more?

Had I had cancer that glorious day with the kids running around my feet, without question, I would have been with them the entire time. No questions asked. No emails returned. No excuses given or expected.

Are you missing it? If you are, please take a moment and live your life as if you have cancer.

MASTERY QUESTIONS

What adjustments can you make in your life to insure that you don't "miss it"?

_____

_____

Chapter 8

·····································

DEALING WITH ADVERSITY—
GET USED TO IT

·····································

THE GREATEST GLORY IN LIVING LIES NOT IN NEVER
FAILING, BUT IN RISING EVERY TIME WE FAIL.
— NELSON MANDELA

Adversity is a way of life. Without it, what is the point? You could never experience the highs if you haven't experienced the lows. View adversity as a typical bell curve. For most of the human race, we live life in the middle, plodding along day to day without too much drama. No real highs and no corresponding lows. But every once in a while, God throws you a curveball so you have to deal with something on the lower end of the spectrum. That's when life gets interesting, and ultimately, when you realize it is all worthwhile. It's a natural law that what goes up must come down. For every great high, there is an equal low. So the higher the high you're bound to experience, there'll be an equally low low. It's very straightforward when you think about it.

My recommendation is to go for the highest highs and

accept the corresponding lows. Because life is short, if you don't experience the greatest on the top end, what's the point? A life of living in the middle of the bell curve? I don't think so. Taking the maximum risk you can take will make for living a more extraordinary life. After all, if your life isn't worth making a movie about once it's over, it must have been pretty dull. Or to put it another way, it's pretty tough to be satisfied being a snail if your desire is to be a bird.

Life is full of dealing with unfortunate gotcha's. Friends and family members die, children are born with challenges, you get fired from your job, you lose money in the stock market; there are illnesses, car wrecks, broken arms or legs, and of course, losing at love. Life will always have bumps in the road, and when you come to one, you must deal with and work your way through it. If you want to continue on your journey, you might be able to go around the bump, or more likely over it, but you can't stand still or you won't be going anywhere. You can't put these bumps "on hold" for another time. They are immediate and must be faced in the now.

If you lose your job, is it the end of your existence or the beginning of a new one? When a loved one dies, is it the end of your life as well or an opening for learning to share others' gifts? Won't a challenged child before you open your eyes to a new perspective? You get to decide. Look for the multitude of opportunities attached to the situation versus wallowing in the past and playing the part of victim. In this role, you cannot move forward.

Getting cancer certainly applies. It sucks in so many ways, and unless you've been on the receiving end of it, no words can describe its emotional and physical implications. Nevertheless, it can also be a blessing. It's up to the person who receives cancer into his or her life to choose the point of view from which to view it. Will it be life or death? You choose and move through it accordingly with your position. Would you prefer to live with it or to die from it? Again, you get to decide the path.

An applicable story arrived in my email not long ago. I love its simplicity for driving home the point I want to make here.

A CARROT, AN EGG, OR COFFEE?

Author Unknown

A young woman went to her mother and told her about her life and how things were so hard for her. She did not know how she was going to make it and wanted to give up. She was tired of fighting and struggling. It seemed that as one problem was solved, a new one arose.

Her mother took her to the kitchen. She filled three pots with water and placed each on a high fire. Soon the pots came to boil. In the first she placed carrots, in the second she placed eggs, and in the last she placed ground coffee beans. She let them sit and boil, without saying a word.

In about twenty minutes, she turned off the burners. She fished the carrots out and placed them in a bowl. She pulled the eggs out and placed them in a bowl.

Then she ladled the coffee out and placed it in a bowl. Turning to her daughter, she said, "Tell me what you see."

"Carrots, eggs, and coffee," the daughter replied.

Her mother brought her closer and asked her to feel the carrots. She did and noted that they were soft. The mother then asked the daughter to take an egg and break it. After pulling off the shell, she observed the hardboiled egg.

Finally, the mother asked the daughter to sip the coffee. The daughter smiled as she tasted its rich aroma. The daughter then asked, "What does it mean, Mother?"

Her mother explained that each of these objects had faced the same adversity: boiling water. Each reacted differently. The carrot went in strong, hard, and unrelenting. However, after being subjected to the boiling water, it softened and became weak. The egg had been fragile. Its thin outer shell had protected its liquid interior, but after sitting through the boiling water, its inside became hardened. The ground coffee beans were unique, however. After they were in the boiling water, they had changed the water.

"Which are you?" she asked her daughter. "When adversity knocks on your door, how do you respond? Are you a carrot, an egg, or a coffee bean?"

Think of this: Which am I? Am I the carrot that seems strong, but with pain and adversity do I wilt and become soft and lose my strength?

Am I the egg that starts with a malleable heart, but changes with the heat? Did I have a fluid spirit, but after a death, a breakup, a financial hardship or some other trial, have I become hardened and stiff? Does my shell look the same, but on the inside am I bitter and tough with a stiff spirit and hardened heart?

Or am I like the coffee bean? The bean actually changes the hot water, the very circumstance that brings the pain. When the water gets hot, it releases the fragrance and flavor. If you are like the bean, when things are at their worst, you get better and change the situation around you. When the hour is darkest and trials are their greatest, do you elevate yourself to another level? How do you handle adversity? Are you a carrot, an egg, or a coffee bean?

May we all be COFFEE.

The sooner you live your life as if you have cancer and be "coffee," the sooner you'll be able to wash adverse situations off your back and put them in their place. Accept them as a part of living and you'll live more every day. Refuse them and fight the inevitable and the opposite is true. It's your choice to make. I highly recommend the former and I believe strongly so will the people around you. It's bound to make for living a more Extraordinary Life.

God will never give you more than you can handle. I just wish He didn't trust us so much.
— **Mother Teresa**

MASTERY QUESTIONS

Think about times of adversity you have faced in your life. Did you end up being a carrot, an egg, or a coffee bean in these situations?

_____

_____

Think about any issues or adversities you are currently facing. How can your response to that adversity make you be like the coffee bean?

_____

_____

Chapter 9

PAYING YOURSELF FIRST

TOO MANY PEOPLE ARE SPENDING MONEY THEY
HAVEN'T EARNED, TO BUY THINGS THEY DON'T WANT,
TO IMPRESS PEOPLE THEY DON'T LIKE.
— WILL SMITH

The other day I was waiting in the reception room of the orthodontist's office while Riley got his teeth tightened. Wires and pliers, you know. The reception room is geared entirely for today's youth, complete with three flat-screen televisions mounted on each wall of the room (one wall had windows so a fourth television couldn't be mounted there). Each TV screen was playing a different show simultaneously. Since there were three, it wasn't feasible to have the audio playing since one would most certainly out do the others. I cannot help wondering how much of my kid's orthodontist bill goes toward recovering the cost of this noiseless hardware.

On the main and largest screen was the latest Pixar animated movie from Disney Studios, *Up*. I had not seen it and knew nothing of the storyline, but I had read the reviews stating it was a "Must see." The film was just beginning when I took notice.

With no sound, I could only grasp the storyline from the visual aspect. The movie began with a young boy who meets a young girl, and from the look of things, they share common interests; both are adventure seekers and explorer wannabes. The opening scene is a time lapse of their lives together for the next sixty or so years. They play together, date, get married, go to work, buy and fix up a house, realize they cannot conceive a child, grow old together, the wife gets sick and dies, and the man is left a curmudgeon to live in solitude, setting up the situation for the rest of the movie.

During this opening sequence, an underlying story is presented. The couple tacks a picture of a faraway destination on the wall—Paradise Falls, a land lost in time. Staying true to childhood explorer roots, Paradise Falls becomes the couple's dream destination to visit someday.

In the middle of the room, the husband and wife put a large glass jar with the label, "Paradise Falls Fund" taped to the outside. Every few moments, they walk by the jar (again over time) and drop change from their pockets into it. As the jar begins to fill, the director cuts to a scene where they are driving down the road in their car when they experience a flat tire. Cut to a hammer breaking the jar and the contents spilling all over the table…savings depleted.

A new jar appears in the next scene, and the viewer sees the same drill as before; over time the jar begins to fill with coins when suddenly we cut again. This time it's the wife who suffers a broken leg and is laid up in the hospital. Another hammer is dropped, the jar is broken, and the savings gone.

Once more the couple starts saving for their dream to arrive at Paradise Falls. A tree falls across the roof of the house, and low and behold, the same hammer, different jar, same result. Savings tapped and used up. Our characters slow down, brown hair turns gray, the Paradise Falls photo on the wall fades and tatters, the wife gets sick, and ultimately, she dies. The man sits alone in his chair, having never reached Paradise Falls.

Being a cartoon, one would think this movie was geared toward the youth. However, the older generation could learn a thing or two from this opening scene since unfortunately, many live their lives this way and never attain their goals due to financial irresponsibility. It's a portrayal I believe all too common in the world today—especially with what I see taking place in America.

Lately, every time I look on the Internet, read the newspaper, listen to the radio, or watch the local and national news, I am astounded by how upside down America is financially. It's truly shocking and goes against everything I was ever taught.

The other night I was watching a syndicated program with a financial pundit out of some renowned school back east. The speaker was stressing that currently over 90% of Americans are broke. He cited the level of credit card debt (over one trillion dollars), the collapse of the housing market (where so many Americans thought they had equity), and the lack of savings in proportion to earnings. He stressed that when you looked at the numbers closely, America is broke and living on borrowed funds.

When I was growing up, if someone didn't have enough money to buy something, he had to forego the purchase. This reality was ingrained in me from as early as I can remember. No such thing as "credit" existed, let alone a "credit card." You either had the money or you didn't. And if the latter, you went without.

My grandparents never would have dreamt of buying anything for which they couldn't pay cash. They even paid cash for their house(s). Granted, houses cost less back then, but it was all relative since people also made far less. My grandparents saved what was needed, however, to make the purchase before extending themselves or putting themselves in any form of financial hardship. Pretty basic model if you ask me, and we would all be experiencing a lot less stress in our lives, and in less trouble financially as a country today, if we all (including the government) still adhered to these simple, common sense principles.

It's surprising to see how some people live, and how little they have stashed away for a rainy day. The number of people in this country today who make a six-figure income yet live paycheck to paycheck is astounding. They have nothing in savings with no plan to change. If they were suddenly to lose their means of income for even a short period, they'd find themselves in some serious world of hurt. They have big houses, leased cars, designer clothes, the latest hairstyle, and not a dime in the bank until the next payday comes around. Read *The Millionaire Next Door* if you don't believe me. It's a great book on the subject.

One of my earliest life lessons from my dad was, "Pay yourself first." Before you buy anything, before you pay your bills, the government, the butcher, the baker, or the candlestick maker, pay yourself. Number one and first and foremost is you. Pay yourself ten percent from every dollar you make. My dad enforced this rule with me from the time I received my first check. Paying myself first became a habit, and one that I believe has made me stronger to this very day. You wouldn't be reading this book had I not followed his rule.

If you instill this practice into yourself from the first dollar you make, you'll never miss the ten cents you pay yourself out of it. You also need to discipline yourself that this money is not touchable except for your direst needs or for some incredibly special goal. It's only to be used as your investment in you.

Life can guarantee you that you will experience some adversity such as a tire blowout, a broken leg, or a tree falling on your house. Unexpected expenses are an absolute certainty.

To diminish the unforeseen experiences, invest in yourself with every paycheck you receive. It's a simple proposition.

Madison Avenue will make certain there will be an endless supply of products and services for you to purchase throughout your life. If you succumb to its desires, you will most certainly join the rest of this country's debt-owing masses who pay a minimum of 25% interest for every purchase they make because they carry a balance on their credit cards they don't pay off at each month's end. So a hundred dollar pair of jeans you charge in reality will cost you a hundred and twenty-five.

When you think of your purchases in this manner, department store sales won't seem so much of a "savings." Sales are no longer a good deal and become easy to avoid. If you don't have the money, you can't afford it. It's a very straightforward philosophy. Pay yourself first and set aside money for another time and place. If you really want that pair of jeans but don't have the money, earn the money first so you can actually make the purchase with money you possess.

Being upside down financially is one of the biggest stress mongers in life. Pick up just about any book on stress and it's in the top two. Check out reasons people get divorced and again, fiscal irresponsibility tops the list. I'm convinced that, for the most part, financial challenges in this country are self-inflicted and easily avoided. If you spend less than you make and pay yourself first, beginning with your first paycheck, you'll help to avert this strain on your life.

To get to "Paradise Falls" is one of life's goals. Being financially responsible and managing your money appropriately will ensure the goal is attained. And paying yourself first plays a huge part in the process. You'll feel a greater sense of accomplishment, and in the long run, help to make certain you live an Extraordinary Life.

PAYING YOURSELF FIRST IN ALL ASPECTS OF LIFE

- Don't want to "Miss It"—your Extraordinary Life that is? Then apply the "paying yourself first" principle to your life and not just your bank account!

- Do you ever feel like you are running on empty? That you have given every last drop of yourself to your job, your business, your friends, your children, but you have forgotten to make a single deposit in you?

- In a very busy world, it's easy to forget you are your greatest investment. Save yourself from leading a life of "excruciating" instead of "extraordinary." Don't "Miss it." Stake the first part of your "kitty" toward taking the time to care for you. So pay yourself first—you are sure to be happier and healthier while making for a better boss, employee, parent, lover, or spouse.

- Paying Yourself First has Everything to do with Work/Life Balance.

- You can run but you can't hide.

- If your finances or percentage of self-care are out of balance, your Life is out of Balance.

- Start by "paying yourself first" and watch the equilibrium return.

Chapter 10

THE HUMAN TOUCH

I HAVE WORKED IN THE MEDICAL FIELD FOR OVER
TWENTY YEARS, AND MUCH OF MY WORK HAS BEEN
WITH PEOPLE BATTLING CANCER. IN THE PROGRAMS
WHERE I HAVE HAD THE OPPORTUNITY TO OFFER
COMPLEMENTARY THERAPIES—SOME TOUCH THERAPIES,
SOME NON-TOUCH, THE TOUCH THERAPIES WIN OUT
HANDS DOWN EVERY TIME.
– PAM KOPPEL, LCSW

As I went through my cancer treatment, another helpful aspect of enduring treatment was seeking out the human touch. I believe heartily in the human touch as a natural healing property. Making sure I received an adequate amount of it was paramount to getting through my cancer treatment and its subsequent side-effects.

Now, I can hear the groans and guffaws in the background when you read "The Human Touch." So for clarification's sake,

I'm going on record that it was all professional in nature and one that would not include any Vice Squad interference.

The human touch is defined by massage therapy, facials, pedicures, manicures, and acupuncture. I made sure I had at least one of these treatments every single week of my cancer treatment. And most weeks, I doubled or tripled up on this wonderful part of the eight weeks. I found it to be a definite help and a break from the action of going to the hospital everyday. And if truth be known, the massages were the very best part and I believe the most healing.

On the subject of healing and human touch, I recall a study I read in *Scientific American* some years ago. It took place at a university library and was conducted on multiple occasions to ensure the outcome received was consistent throughout the process.

The study was simple. It consisted of checkout people and an interviewer. The checkout people were first asked to act as librarians and check out patrons' books, but under no circumstances whatsoever, were they to touch the library patrons. The patrons who checked out the books were then interviewed as they left the library. When asked, "How was your visit to the library today?" in more than 90% of the cases where the person was not touched, the reply was equivalent to, "Nothing special."

Next, the opposite was administered. The checkout person had to make physical contact with a touch to the hand or arm as the patron with the books was exiting the checkout area. Same question ensued, "How was your visit to the library today?" This time in over 90% of the cases, the reply was along the lines of, "It was a nice, special, or good experience."

As mentioned, the research team administered this test over and over, and each time, it came back with similar and consistent results. Appropriate human touch made a positive difference on the simplest of undertakings.

I, for one, firmly believe in the human touch and the power of its healing capabilities. Touch someone and see if it brightens up his or her day. I believe you'll be amazed by the result.

THE EXTRAORDINARY POWER OF HUMAN TOUCH

How can anyone dispute the extraordinary influence that human touch plays in healing? From the time our mothers kissed our first skinned elbow to make it feel better it has been clear. Those who fail to see the importance and the power that resides in human touch certainly missed it!

Think about how many times human touch had made a difference to you, in a sad or a joyful moment, a squeeze of the hand, a hug, a pat on the back, or a meaningful and firm handshake. Now payback that meaning by sharing the power of human touch with others.

Chapter 11

FINDING SUCCESS

THE MORE I PRACTICE THE LUCKIER I GET.
– BEN HOGAN

One of the best ways for me to highlight the topic of "Finding Success" is to use one of my favorite subjects as a backdrop. That would be the game of golf. I believe the game provides one of life's greatest metaphor platforms. Golf requires focus, tenacity, perseverance, creativity, imagination, integrity, stability, confidence, and a host of other finely tuned traits. It mirrors executive business requirements on every front. It's so telling that if you ever want to know someone, play a round of golf with him or her. It's the greatest resume to a person's soul that I know.

Golf has played a significant part in my life, not only in the enjoyment of being with a group of family members or friends, but also in business. I think golf is wonderful, and I cannot stress enough the importance this "game" has played in shaping my worldview.

The game of golf and I made our formal acquaintance in 1965 when I was nine. I recall playing croquet with my friends in the front yard of our North Seattle home one spring evening while my parents watched from the front porch. I must have been waxing the competition as my mother turned to my father and said, "I bet Randy would like to learn to play golf."

My Grandpa Jack had golfed most of his life, and in his eighties, he was able to shoot his age on occasion at his local senior community golf course near Portland, Oregon. My folks collectively determined it would be a good thing to have my grandfather become my golfing mentor.

Grandpa Jack was a stern but gentle man of English heritage. And he was all business on the course. In my naiveté to the sport, and during an early round in my career with Grandpa Jack when he parted the fairway for the fifth or sixth straight hole, I quipped, "Wow, what luck." He turned quickly and deliberately, sized me up, looked me square in the eye and said, "That's not luck, son; that's skill." I made a point thereafter to keep my golf-related comments to myself during rounds with him unless I first gave deep thought to what I was saying.

Dad simultaneously took up the game. Grandpa purchased a used two-dollar ladies four iron and a putter for me that he pulled from the bin at the local golf retailer. At the same time, my dad got a brand new full set of left-handed Wilson irons for himself. I bellowed a bit about only having one mediocre hitting club in my possession since I figured I was sorely at a disadvantage with so few weapons in my arsenal. But Grandpa insisted on instructing me to learn how to hit that club and use it for every shot (except to putt) on the course for the first year of my play.

That lesson was the first and still the best I received in my introduction to the game. I share this tactic to this day with every beginning golfer I come into contact. It's funny, but not many follow this advice because they always want to hit that big driver long before they have a clue about how to make it work. But I'm convinced that Grandpa Jack's advice was sound for the novice player, especially if you don't play a lot but find yourself playing in a corporate tournament four people scramble. Then the skill you acquired is certain to make you a hit with your playing partners.

Personally, I took to golf like a duck to water and played everyday during the summer from seventh grade until high school graduation. At a minimum, I played thirty-six holes a day and many times up to forty-five. To this day, I contend that I would have probably ended up in prison were it not for golf. Golf provided an outlet for me and my friends that made us compete on a daily basis for quarters instead of unsuspecting neighbors' hubcaps or whatever else we would have conjured up to vandalize or steal.

As with most things, the more one practices, the better skill set one obtains, and for that reason, I have always loved Ben Hogan's quote, "The more I practice, the luckier I get." Putting forth time and the desire produces results. I won the junior men's club championship at our course three straight years and moved up a division each year. Playing varsity on the high school golf team led to a golf scholarship at a Washington State Community College, renowned for its golf program.

All told, I am extremely grateful to my parents' foresight and my subsequent desire to learn the game early in my life.

My understanding of golf's basics and learning proper course etiquette proved invaluable in my professional life. I put to work the ability to build more business relationships and cut more deals on the course than any other means or venue. And it's always great fun to play, especially when you win.

Back in the year 2000, my father-in-law, Bud, invited me to be his partner at his local club's annual member/guest tournament—the "Rainier Cup." The tournament was then and continues to be the club's biggest annual tournament with full club participation year in and year out.

Keeping score in golf is all about who shoots the lowest score, or about matching yourself against the course. The Rainier Cup, however, is different in regards to how the match is scored. In lieu of having the lowest score, this format is exactly the opposite. The team strives to have the highest score because the game is played over three eighteen hole days and is based on a point system. Of course, the team members need to shoot their very best, and points are allocated based upon aces, eagles, birdies, pars, and bogies. Anything above a bogie garners no points, and thus, is no help in getting the team to the winner's circle. Club handicaps are included in the scoring process, so any players without a USGA established handicap will not be admitted to the playing field.

In addition to playing to achieve the team's name etched onto the "Cup" to be on display for all members to see in the club's trophy case, there are the side bets. Every year, Bud had his crib sheet. He would walk from member to member on the front end and make side bets. The typical bet was known as "three-fives," which consists of five dollars for each nine, plus another five bucks for the overall round of eighteen. Each person is playing against each team on an individual basis for fifteen dollars each day of the tournament. Each individual compares his first nine holes, then the second, and lastly the total eighteen to determine how much of the fifteen dollars he actually wins or loses.

Because Bud is the outgoing jovial character he is, everyone in the club always wants a "piece" of Bud. During that tournament, he gladly accepted the challenge because the event was almost as much about betting with his member chums as about the notoriety of cup ownership.

Three-fives might not seem like much, but when you do the math over three days with seventy-some teams, you're talking about some serious money. All bets are settled before you leave the event after dinner on Sunday night, and if you play poorly, you could be reaching into your pocket for a grand or so "each." Counter that with a win and the upside is upwards of three or four thousand for the team. Going in, I had no idea such high stakes were on the table.

Bud was a true twenty-something handicapper, but he had the capacity to catch fire on a moment's notice. Having a handicap in the twenties and the ability to throw in a round in the mid-eighties makes for a good playing partner. I, on the other hand, was at best at this time a ten, but every once in awhile, I could throw in a few sequential pars and an outside birdie. Usually, one could pretty much count on me shooting in the low eighties on a consistent basis.

At the end of the tournament's first day, we topped the leader board as we put together two solid rounds between us.

Being in front on the first day is not a bad place to be in any aspect of life. However, I have always preferred to be just below the top or under the radar, and then to come from behind, opposed to holding the pole position and setting the bar for all to take a shot at. I'm not sure why, but that's always been my dogma. Nevertheless, I left the course that night feeling pretty good about having topped the field on the first day of this all important and meaningful club tournament. Bud and I also had done pretty well on the "crib" sheet, although I hadn't the remotest idea about it since Bud had taken care of it entirely behind the scenes, and it was tightly tucked in his pocket.

Day two arrived and nerves set in as we gave a few back to the field and removed ourselves from the top tier position. We were still on the plus side (remember it was about total points vs. low score). In this format, if you ended day two on the plus side, you had a shot at the title. Not much ground is left to pick up as long as you stay in the plus column since history had proven that the winning score typically fell between plus six to nine. If you hit the top number, you most likely proved your team was a sand bagger since such a high score was seldom reached. The lower number was typically the case and closer to the tournament's intention. At the second day's end, we were at plus three with the final round to play.

With a full field tournament on one course, in order for everyone to finish in a timely fashion and allow everyone to mingle following, a shotgun start is required. This format requires everyone in the field to go to a specific hole on the course with two foursomes on each tee. When the gun sounds, the first foursome tees off, followed by the second group once the first foursome is out of shot range. We had drawn the third hole as our start, one of the shorter par fours on the course. It required a good tee shot from a placement standpoint in order to have a decent shot made into the elevated, narrow, and heavily bunkered green. Could I have picked any hole on the course to start, this one was in the top three.

For the next fourteen holes, we held our own, not setting anything on fire but keeping ourselves in contention without too many holes blanking points. After we teed off on eighteen and rode up the fairway, I turned to Bud to ask him where we stood. Bud always had the pencil on the course since he was the consummate business partner in such matters. He did some quick math and then stated, "We each have to score points in our final three holes (remember we started on number three) to have any chance at winning this thing." I looked straight at him and said, "We can do that. I'll par in, you bogey in, and we're there."

In most rounds or tournaments I have ever played, I never wanted to know what I needed to shoot or cared where my opponents stood. I always thought knowing the score got in the way since golf is all about hitting one shot at a time, not a hole or series of holes. Focusing on what you need to accomplish is almost certain death and opens the door to losing your focus on the task before you—the next shot you have to make. Ask any touring pro, and he'll most certainly concur.

At that moment though, in the middle of the eighteenth fairway, I wanted to know because I needed to get my bearings and set a goal. I had hit a good drive and had about a hundred yards between the hole and me. Bud was in good shape as well. The green on eighteen is two-tiered with a steep hill that divides it front from back. The pin on the final round was positioned on the lower half and in the best location on the green for my game. The shot I envisioned in my head was for the ball to land just over the flag on the slope of the green and then funnel back for a short uphill putt. The shot was struck and landed exactly as I envisioned it. The only exception being that it hit right on the crest of the hill as planned but stayed put. It didn't roll down, and thus, it left me a steep and slippery downhill putt of some fourteen to sixteen feet. I couldn't believe it as Rainier's greens were rolling about eleven on the stimpmeter that day.

Downhill putts of this nature are about the same as setting a golf ball on the coffee table in your home and then tipping the table up on one side. It's that fast as the greens had been double cut and rolled, making them lightning quick. When I surveyed the shot before me, I couldn't believe the ball stayed where it did; all I had to do was blow on it, and by the time it reached the hole, it would be traveling faster than walking speed. All I could do was line the ball up, touch it with the putter face, sit back, and hitch my wagon for the ride. If the ball didn't hit the hole, I was certain to have a putt of equal length or more coming back. I took dead aim, focused my breathing, and touched the ball as planned.

The ball rolled true, gained speed as imagined, hit dead center, hopped a bit straight up in the air, and dropped back down into the hole and disappeared. Birdie! Bud made his bogie, and then we headed to our second to last hole with smiles on our faces and adrenalin flowing through our veins.

Bud made more bogies while I made pars on the remaining two holes—goal not only accomplished but exceeded. As we headed back to the clubhouse, Bud was grinning ear to ear with pencil in hand. I must admit, I was wearing a pretty wide smile myself. We obviously had no idea where we stood with respect to the rest of the field, but our smiles were earned from having finished in the manner we had by setting our objective and then meeting it, thus making the final day extraordinary.

Bud was an ardent and multi-talented individual who could simultaneously drive the cart, do the math, and still put it all down on the card. By the time we arrived at the scorer's table, he had it all figured out. We had scored plus seven and a half for the tournament and as fate would have it, we had won the tournament by half a point.

The celebration that ensued that evening was second to none in my experience. Few things in life feel so good as winning—especially with how we finished the last three holes just a short time before. It was wonderful on all fronts.

I'm still not exactly sure what was more enjoyable—watching Bud run around the dining room collecting our crib sheet bets, poking fun at all those on the losing end, or just sitting in the glow of the moment and absorbing the joy of our success. It all melded together the instant I overheard Bud say to his best friend, "Wes, this win was better than sex."

Arnold Palmer once stated that he would rather win one tournament than have a hundred top ten finishes. Before that day, I didn't understand his position since one win would not make him as much money as all those top ten finishes. But following my and Bud's triumph that day, I completely got what he meant.

Winning changes everything about one's psyche. It's completely different than being pretty good or almost the best. When you're on top, you feel unbeatable, and you carry that feeling of invincibility with you for the rest of your life. No matter the situation, you can summon up the memory of your success and draw upon it as an emotional boost whenever you need it. I cannot stress enough the emotional boost that victory brings.

Once you win, you always feel, "I've done this before, and I know for a fact I can do it again." Henry Ford's famous line, "Whether you think you can or you think you can't, you're right" certainly pertains. Once you're on the top, you realize you possess the ability to come through when it counts—over and over and over again because you now have an inner voice telling you that you can make that shot since you've done it before. That's an enormous arrow to have in your quiver!

Making that "shot" and experiencing an ultimate win relates to every aspect of your life, even if it's something as miniscule (in the bigger scheme of things) as winning a club championship. You can only be as good as the best thing you'll ever do. I'm convinced of that everyday. You don't have to wait to get cancer to realize it's the case.

Bud told me years later, "Winning that tournament was unexpected. I didn't enter it thinking we'd win. But it was the best thing as a golfer I ever experienced." When I asked him, "Better than getting your hole-in-one?" he replied, "Yes, even better than my hole-in-one." I've never had a hole-in-one, so I'll just take his word for it.

Chapter 12

BELIEVING
IN MIRACLES

I'M A REALIST—I EXPECT MIRACLES.
— DR. WAYNE DYER

A few years and a score ago, my family experienced a Christmas like none prior. It was to be the first Christmas without my maternal grandmother, Opal. "Nanny," as we called her, was an angel who had walked the earth, and Christmas wasn't Christmas without her bigger-than-life presence in our family.

Throughout my childhood, I could always count on Nanny to BE the holidays. When we walked in her house, the smell of the season permeated the air; evergreen from the freshly cut tree, scented candles, pumpkin and mince pies, gingerbread, roast, and biscuits filled the air, all highlighted by Nanny and her husband Bill's warm and friendly manner. It was the most glorious time of year for a youth with all the dreams of Christmas joy to come buzzing around the room and between my ears. One could barely sit still with anticipation.

I would have traded fifteen trips to the circus then and now for one Christmas at Nanny's. I am extremely fortunate that for the first twenty-five years of my life, I never experienced a Christmas without Nanny's divine presence mingled in with all the holiday fixings.

Nanny wasn't more than five feet and she tipped the scale just a bit over a hundred. But pound for pound, I would put her up against anyone when it came to working manual labor around the house. She was a twister on steroids. My great-uncle used to say, "Just put a broom in her hand and she'll be happy." He couldn't have been more right. The only time she sat still during the day was to watch "her" show "General Hospital"—at 3 p.m. Audrey and Steve Hardy were the order of the day; no matter what was in the wash or on the counter, it could wait. "General Hospital" was sacred.

When it came to caring for kids or wildlife, Nanny had no peer. I recall as a young child visiting her home in Tacoma, when Nanny and Bill took in a neighbor girl for the day. The little girl had been home with her babysitter, but she found her way to my grandparents' home to be on the receiving end of warm milk and cookies. She then slept there for the better part of the afternoon. Much to my grandparents' dismay, the girl's sitter never once sought her out. My grandparents were beside themselves, and they thought the sitter, mother, father, aunt, uncle, or whoever else might remotely be in charge, should be incarcerated for neglect.

My grandmother fed the squirrels, Stellar Jays, neighbors' animals, and anything else with feathers or fur that happened into the yard. She even had a pet crow she fed everyday at the same time—you could set your watch by his arrival.

About the only thing that didn't belong in this world as far as Nanny was concerned was a snake, slug, or mouse. Other than that, all was part of her and God's world, and she would do whatever it took to ensure they made it through to another day with a full belly.

At the holidays, Nanny was a genius at buying presents. Every year, she always found gifts that were so incredibly special you could never anticipate what she would give you. It always suited you remarkably. It was never something on your list but when you received it, you realized it was something you needed or wanted such as a perfectly fitting sweater. Giving gifts was truly one of Nanny's specialties, and I never figured out how she knew exactly what would bring that "Ahh" moment when we unwrapped our gifts while nestled around the tree. Her gifts were truly special on so many fronts.

My twenty-sixth Christmas, however, would not to be the same. We had lost Nanny earlier that year to cancer, and now the magical glowing holiday season was dark and forlorn. There would be no smells, no joy and laughter, no mince and pumpkin pies, no waiting anxiously by the tree for her to finish up the dishes and appear, and none of those special gifts. It was as if the air had been completely sucked out of the world, leaving me completely alone for the first time in my life.

My parents made other plans that year to be away for the holidays. My sister lived in California and was staying put. It was unspoken among us, yet it was the loudest din imaginable with a resounding scream of "We can't be together" because it would just be too incredibly painful to attempt the unimaginable—a Christmas without Nanny.

To compound matters, I was traveling for work a considerable amount leading up to the holiday break. I vividly recall flying into Seattle the last few days before Christmas and looking out the airplane's window at the black and lifeless city. It was the emptiest feeling I had ever experienced. I prayed the plane would never land because I couldn't bear the thought of walking in the cold and damp to my empty car and driving home to a listless and holiday free house.

Before leaving Los Angeles, I had the wherewithal to go to the cash machine and withdraw my Christmas gift money since I had not yet made a single purchase. I was prolonging the inevitable and avoiding all aspects of the season until its final and unbearable moment. But this one action made me feel good because I knew that with all of the emotion stirring, the fewer activities required once I got home, the better.

As I approached my dark and empty house, I stopped at the mailbox to gather a week's worth of holiday mail. It was stuffed with every imaginable flyer to gobble up the cash I had previously garnered. An absolute mess was strewn upon my kitchen table as well as the contents from my travel pockets. I went to bed, closed my eyes, and pretended the hurt wasn't real.

The next morning, I set out to do my shopping and attempted to put myself in the holiday spirit. It was short-lived. I couldn't find the cash I had procured the day prior to streamline my shopping efforts. I literally tore the house apart looking for it—under the cushions of every seat, every room, every pocket, the washer, and the dryer. I even looked in the oven. No cash—it was not to be found. I screamed at the top of my lungs in utter frustration, but still, no cash fell from the sky. I was toast, and it only added insult to injury as I headed out with my list shortened and scaled back.

For the next week, I sulked. The only break in my morose attitude was to rampage through the house one more time in a fit of rage, trying my damnedest to locate the lost funds. I knew they had to be there because I never lost things, especially not money, and I knew I'd had it when I walked into the house.

I sat in the chair in the living room, staring out the window, and suddenly felt myself filling with rage. I leapt from my chair, throwing the cushion against the wall, and cursed God at the top of my lungs for being so unjust! How could He not only take the most beautiful person in this world, a living angel, in the most painful and excruciating way possible, but on top of it, heap the pain and despair upon me at this most sensitive time of year. "I hate YOU, God. I HATE YOU!" I cried. My rage transcended into sorrow and I wept uncontrollably for what seemed to be forever.

A knock at the door snapped me back to consciousness. I walked by the window, looked out, and saw a dilapidated Volkswagen Bug in the driveway. It had no front fenders, was-two toned (primer gray and yellow), and was missing a passenger side window, which had been replaced with saran wrap.

When I opened the door, before me stood a young man in his late twenties, unshaven, with long dirty blond hair, holes in his jeans, and a long-sleeved undershirt with the sleeves rolled up. Having no idea what this guy wanted from me, I looked at him with disdain. Whatever he wanted, I had no intention of buying. "May I help you?" I barked from behind the screen door. He looked me straight in the eye with his dark sunken lids, reached into his pocket, and pulled out my cash. Then he asked, "Did you really want to throw this away? I'm your garbage man, and I found this in your garbage. I thought you might want it back."

I was mostly speechless, but I did have the wherewithal to offer him a reward for being so thoughtful and forthright. This nameless person looked at me deeply, smiled, and said, "No, my reward is being able to return it to you." Then he walked to his car, started it up, and puttered away. I never saw him again.

The next few hours I spent on my knees begging God for forgiveness. I realized I had held so little faith in HIM that now I was ashamed. I knew better, but in my moment of agony, I forgot all the goodness I had learned over the years. A true miracle had presented itself, and I couldn't help but believe my grandmother played a huge part in creation and lobbying with God. She had sent me my gift.

Miracles are all around us everyday. All we have to do is to be open to them and allow them to be recognized. According to the doctors, I'm beating the odds just by being alive to write this story. That's a miracle in and of itself. Living your life as if you have cancer will only serve to open your eyes and heart to such wonder.

MASTERY QUESTIONS

Refresh your memory. Have you experienced a Miracle?

_____

_____

If so, how has that experience enhanced your life as Extraordinary?

_____

_____

Chapter 13

SOCIAL OBSERVATION

Think? Why think!
We have computers to do that for us.
— Jean Rostand

Yesterday, I had the extreme pleasure of accompanying my kids on their weekly ski excursion via the school district's after-school ski bus program. How things have changed since I partook in this activity some forty-plus years ago.

As I arrived with my gear to join my kids, I saw the row of yellow buses just as they used to be lined up when I went on the school ski bus—nice and neatly rowed with hard gleaming green naugahyde vinyl uncomfortable seats. I could even smell the remnants of some kid's three-week-old vomit permeating the air.

I was taken aback when my kids, donning their packs, informed me these were NOT the modes of transportation WE were going to be using to get us to the slopes. In fact, they had a look of disdain over my even considering that we might venture onto such a vehicle to go skiing. No, those busses were merely for the kids being transported home.

Low and behold, next appeared a luxury coach deemed suitable for the skiers' needs. The rig came complete with a drop down multi-screen DVD playback (throughout the cabin), hi-back comfy seats, overhead lights and blowers, and an onsite bathroom in the rear. The heat was also adjustable throughout the interior so you had the opportunity to adjust your regulator if it were too hot or cold, just as if you were taking a tour through the Alps with your personal tour guide. Sweetness. I have to admit I was instantly impressed and let it pass as such!

To add to the comforts, the lead chaperone came equipped with a sealed case of bottled waters, cokes, and chocolate chip cookies as snacks for the après ski ride back to civilization.

From a social standpoint, another observation was the use of IPOD's and cellular phones. Many kids had headphones in their ears (even with the movie *Night at the Museum* playing in the background), thus effectively eliminating any social contact with their peers. As I recall, socializing was one of the highlights of my Junior High ski bus experience—especially if a girl I liked happened to be on the same bus. Not so with your earphones plugged in tightly and your head facing forward. Solitude is the name of this game.

As we reached a milepost on the way home, the lead chaperone got on the bus microphone (another nuance) and let the travelers know they should expect to be back at the school for pick up within fifteen minutes; thus, make any arrangements (i.e. call Mom, Dad, nanny, or caretaker) to pick you up accordingly. It worked—as we drove onto the school grounds, we were perfectly in line with the stream of SUV's coming in front and behind as if on parade. How wonderfully convenient!

I know this new, young and technological world has been occurring all around me for years. I guess I just didn't realize the complete social ramifications of these wonderful electronic devices and luxurious improvements to our lives until it hit me in one short sitting. Exactly when all these changes took place for getting our kids to and from the slopes, I'm not sure. Overtime, no doubt, and I guess if I'd had children right after I graduated from high school, it would be less noticeable to me because it would have been more gradual. Instead, I waited many years to have children so the comparison between my and my children's ski trips was almost like a jolt into the future.

No wonder today's youth have shorter attention spans, and they feel the need for getting it all now, not later? No wonder they don't want to pick berries in the summer or flip burgers in the winter, or that a teenager will flip out without his or her IPOD, PlayStation, XBox, Wii, or without access to MySpace, YouTube, and the Internet. Have you been on the receiving end of a teen whose cell phone is about to go dead, and the charger is nowhere to be found? I have and it isn't pretty.

This subject certainly can be expounded upon further, and I'm sure countless XGen professional sociologists study and chronicle this behavior change continually. It is not my intention to come across as *old* here (even though I did turn fifty-four today). And my point isn't to drive home the "When I was a boy, I walked to school uphill both ways in the snow." I am certainly not bashing having a more comfortable means to get to the slopes. I'm sure the nice bus ride is well-intentioned.

My purpose here is purely one of observation and to share my thoughts on one particular change in the social upbringing of today's youth compared to during my own. As our children's parents, teachers, and life guides, we enable them to expect everything without the necessary responsibility required to get it. Having the latest and greatest new gadgets has become almost an expected rite of passage. And I plead guilty here as a parent. But we make it so easy. What happened to personal management training, such as remembering to bring your own snack and drink? If you forget, you go without. And what about learning to interact, be polite, and speak to the person next to you? Heaven forbid I don't have a phone, IPOD, or video playing to keep me occupied! You mean I HAVE to talk to you?

I am aware my parents probably had something similar to voice about my generation when I was my children's age. Seeing the differences in how each generation is raised is inevitable. And determining whether progress has been made lies in the eye of the beholder.

What happens though when it's not? The real test will be when our children are faced with the reality of making a life for themselves in the real world. When the snacks are no longer provided and the video isn't running to keep their minds pacified. I wonder where that will take them. Or will we as a generation continue to provide these "necessities" without a cost? I don't believe so because everything has a cost. At least that's what I was brought up to believe.

It appears we're headed on a collision course of asking "Is it live, or is it Memorex?"

If you can remember that last line, you're old enough to understand where I'm coming from.

DON'T MISS IT:
PULL YOUR HEAD OUT OF YOUR **ASS**ESSORIES

I love the personal and professional opportunities that have come from the Internet. This explosion has been literally a worldwide gift to our generation and the generations that will follow. Now truly anything is possible. That includes the book you hold in your hand; its authors reside on separate sides of the country, with the various individuals who were so crucial in its production strewn throughout different locations, all providing different services yet all in communication through the Internet. Dare I say, it's Extraordinary!

But with change and advances of any kind, come transitions, adjustments, and fallout. We have not stopped playing with our technology, our "new toys" long enough to notice what if any toll has ensued on our relationships and our personal beings. It is no surprise to me that many people are feeling disconnected in a generation of 24/7 connectivity. We have created a world with no closing hour, no Work/Life boundaries—literally, Google never ends or sleeps.

Does this apply to you? How do you spend your time? What would your life be like without today's technological advances? How often are you checking your e-mail each day? Really take a minute to think about your "relationship" with your TV, computers, your PDA, BlackBerry, I-Phone, cell phone, techno toys, and electronic gizmos. How much time do you spend with your electronic gadgets?

For many to find balance, it took an active choice to pull their heads out of their <u>assessories</u> to create boundaries, and to set limits regarding where, when, and for what duration of time they will use their computer devices.

Many of us refuse to see a problem exists. "Everyone else is 'over-using' but not me," "If I stop I will lose and someone else will win." And "I'm really not that bad." This cycle mirrors the behavior of those who suffer from addiction or lives dictated by fear, potentially leaving you regretful for having "missed" your life and certainly many of the most Extraordinary, rich, and meaningful moments that make up your life.

Technology and all its magic will continue to make mind-<u>bloggling</u> accelerated advances. As it does, we will be grateful, but nonetheless, let us also be mindful to try harder to stay connected face to face, savoring each-other as live individuals, and feeling the physicality of communication in the flesh. The key is in taking the time to assess how you can use technology to enhance your life while still not missing your life.

I have often pondered that our most imminent danger may someday come from above, but no one will notice because we are all looking down. Look Up! That is where Extraordinary begins.

MASTERING YOUR EXTRAORDINARY LIFE

Seeking Life Balance?

- Consider hanging an open and closed sign on your phone and computer.

- Our love affair with technology is deep. Most relationships take work, are not always easy, and often come with complications. Why should our "relationship" with our coveted technology be any different? That being said, ask yourself the following question:

- Does this close "relationship" you share with your technology make your life more or less Extraordinary?

- In what ways has technology enhanced your life?

- In what ways has technology diminished your life?

- What changes you can implement regarding your computer devices in order to increase your daily satisfaction?

....

Chapter 14

SELLING IT

....

DON'T WAIT FOR EXTRAORDINARY OPPORTUNITIES. SEIZE
COMMON OCCASIONS AND MAKE THEM GREAT. WEAK MEN
WAIT FOR OPPORTUNITIES; STRONG MEN MAKE THEM.
– ORISON SWETT MARDEN

Nothing happens until something is sold. Sales are on the forefront of every business transaction because without the sale, there is nothing to service or produce. Sales keep everyone else in the organization employed because without sales, there is no business. It's funny but the job description of being in sales still carries one of the most negative connotations in the professional world. Insurance, real estate, mattresses, and used cars fall under the categories that help to blemish the profession. In my opinion it's too bad sales has gained this bad name because I believe sales is one of the world's very top professions. For me, it has always been and always will be at the forefront of what makes the world an extraordinary environment in which to do business.

Zig Ziglar, the infamous sales coach, teaches in his seminars the importance of salespeople and the seriousness of being a qualified and professional salesperson. He states that being in sales is the greatest profession because it is recession proof and provides the best job security in the world. If you can sell, you'll always be employed because there are always opportunities for competent and qualified salespeople. I completely concur; after all, it's the salespeople who create the revenue and keep the machine humming.

One of the first requirements of selling is getting your "pitch" down. Whatever you're selling, you must be able quickly and succinctly to cover your topic in a convincing and clear manner. I have been privy to thousands of sales pitches in my life, and as with everything else, I've witnessed the good, the bad, and the indifferent. By the way, if it falls under the latter, it falls under "bad." One of the very best presentations I ever had the pleasure of participating in was in Barcelona at the Formula One race. We were doing a relationship-marketing program for our Global Account customer, and we had invited Jackie Stewart of Formula One racing fame to come to the suite and give us a "talk." Jackie was in charge of the Jaguar Formula One car (which Ford owned at the time), and Ford was a customer of the Global Account team—thus the tie-in.

Jackie stood in the middle of the room (in his British Green Jaguar Racing jacket and cap). Although he was not a large man in stature, he quickly filled the room with his presence and Scottish brogue accent. His presentation was flawless from start to finish without a single pause, "uh," or "um." He squared himself front and center and proceeded to give a case study oration on how he "closed" HSBC into becoming the main sponsor of the Jaguar Formula One Race Team. His presentation was brilliant, filled with timely anecdotes, inflections, and of course an uplifting and crescendo building finale. He addressed the entire room, but his target was our client's Senior Vice President, who most certainly had the means and wherewithal to put an additional logo on Jackie's sleeve. I only wish I had a recording of this presentation because it would certainly garner thousands of views on YouTube. It was that good, and if ever there were an example to put in front of a group of sales trainees, this presentation was an instructor's dream come true.

Not everyone has the charisma and capabilities of a Jackie Stewart, but if you're in sales, it's mandatory to use what you have and to make it work. A good example is the following story I stumbled across. I titled it *The Sales Pitch*. It's clear, to the point, and demonstrates how to make it easy for your clients quickly to understand the benefits of your offering.

> Airman Jones was assigned to the induction center where he was to advise new recruits about their government benefits, especially their GI insurance. It wasn't long before Captain Smith noticed that Airman Jones had almost a 100% record for insurance sales, which had never happened before. Rather than ask about this, the Captain stood in the back of the room and listened to Jones' presentation.
>
> Jones explained the basics of the GI Insurance program to the new recruits, and then said, "If you have GI Insurance and go into battle and are killed, the government has to pay $200,000 to your beneficiaries. If you don't have GI insurance, and you go into battle and get killed, the

government has to pay a maximum of $6,000."

"Now," he concluded," which groups do you think are going to be sent into battle first?"

Another big part of being successful in sales usually requires sound negotiation skills. Hundreds of great books and CDs exist on the topic so I will not bore you with specifics. I'd much rather refer you to the proper resources of chosen books or learned individuals on the subject. From this source, you can better understand the specifics of involving a buyer and seller, and knowing the investment of time and energy required to work through a successful negotiation. I prefer to focus on the macro level of a successful negotiation and understand the value of focusing your attention on creating a win-win scenario between opposing parties.

When my daughter Emily was about seven years old, she entered into one of the more memorable and successful negotiations I was privy to in her young life. It was between her and her then six-year old brother. Emily wanted to go for the day to Wild Waves Park some thirty miles from our house. It would be a full day of sun, fun, and getting wet, and it was something she very much wanted to do that week. But her brother had a different idea for a day well spent—going to the park with his friends. Since they were out of school for the summer and I was working, there was no way we were going to be able to split them up. It was an all-or-nothing state of affairs. I looked closely at my daughter and explained that the only way Wild Waves was going to happen would be if both she and Riley agreed on the course of events. Within seconds, I could see the wheels of machination at work in her active head. She was a young girl on a very specific mission from that moment forward.

She trapped her brother, cornered him so he had no escape, and proceeded to expound the virtues of spending a day at Wild Waves versus going to some park with his friends where there would be no frills. Wild Waves had slides, water, speed, excitement, candy corn, sun, and of course his friends could be invited as well. Her positioning was relentless and focused entirely on how, by going to Wild Waves, HE would have the best day he could possibly hope to expect for the entire summer vacation. On top of that, Wild Waves cost money and the park he wanted to go to was free. Thus, he could go to that park any time he wanted since it wouldn't be a big deal for Mom or Dad to take him there. Wild Waves, on the other hand, was exclusive and carried a value he wouldn't realize from any old public park. Those weren't her exact words, mind you, but the message was succinct.

Riley looked at her intently and nodded his head, but he didn't bite completely since he definitely had already locked on to what he had previously envisioned. Emily continued, "Riley, if we go to Wild Waves this week, you'll be able to do whatever you want the rest of the week because Mom and Dad will make sure that happens. Wild Waves is a once in a lifetime, and we won't be able to do it again this summer. Your friends will have a great time. And that park you want to go to will still be there whenever, but Wild Waves is only for a short time. Remember, it closes in September, and we'll be back in school then anyway." The sales pitch was non-ending as over and over she reiterated the benefit HE would receive by going versus what he'd be giving up for only a short time. Thus, very little sacrifice with an upside potential far greater than any average "park." While she continued to focus on the benefit for "Riley," it was really ALL about Emily and what SHE wanted the outcome to be. Her brother was engaged, listening, and absorbing the pitch, and eventually, he did buy in—hook, line, and sinker. When he did surrender his position to go along with her proposition, it was because she had SOLD him on Wild Waves being the better deal.

Emily quickly turned to me, outlining the obvious result (which I had so cheerfully witnessed), and she made sure we were in sync and all onboard for our trek to Wild Waves. She wanted to make sure to solidify the deal and receive one hundred percent buy-in without the remote chance of a refund. As I say, it was a masterful execution at a very tender age of exactly how to execute a proper negotiation.

She had not only gotten what she wanted, but she had ensured that her opponent felt he had won as well. She reiterated after the fact that he had made the proper choice by outlining a few of the key points so he felt happy with his decision. It wasn't over the top like some sales pitches I've witnessed where the salesperson didn't know when to shut up after closing the deal. It simply had the perfect amount of reassurance that he had made a good buying decision. Emily added just enough dressing to ensure there wouldn't be an ounce of buyer's remorse on his salad. The outcome produced a complete and utter win-win proposition for both participating parties.

I doubt Emily entered the negotiation with all these thoughts planned out in her mind, but she was wise enough to understand the ramifications as she moved forward; she realized at the outset that she would not get her way unless she had 100% compliance from the other party. And in that moment, I realized my daughter possessed the necessary instincts for survival in a world where negotiation is an everyday requirement.

There's an old adage, "You never get what you're worth; you only get what you negotiate." There's a fair amount of truism in that saying—I know from partaking in its ramifications on numerous occasions. It's important to hold fast to your "worth" while at the same time you are empathetic to your adversary's position. If you fail fully to understand the other's position, you will ultimately lose. Maybe not in the immediate sense, but over time, you're bound to get the bad end of the deal. I believe strongly in this mantra as it boils down to the basic laws of nature.

A couple of years ago, my close friend Austin passed away. He was my surrogate father and I loved him dearly. I know he loved me on equal terms, but part of our relationship was to fight like cats and dogs over what we each believed was right versus wrong. In all of our arguments, I never "won." He was hell-bent on being right, and in his mind, he was always so with absolutely zero bend in his positions. With him, I am certain I was the same. One night, my son Riley and I were invited to his house for dinner. During the evening, our conversation inevitably progressed into one of our more heated "chats" until it became explosive with Austin taking an opposing view to one of my "positions." When Riley and I departed, I asked my son how he felt about what had transpired throughout the evening. Riley looked at me and said, "Well, one thing I learned tonight, Dad, is no one is ever going to win an argument with Austin." Riley was only eleven when he gave me this bit of advice.

Austin had been a purchasing agent his entire professional life for a major aerospace company located in the Seattle area. His total being was all about "negotiation" of the very best deal he could obtain for himself and his company. After all his raises, merit recognitions, and advancements, his personal self-esteem always boiled down to how well he performed the task at hand. He was committed to making sure he negotiated the very best deal, and he was determined to do so. He worked in this capacity for over thirty years, so he had a lot of experience in the world of getting what he wanted and on his own terms. After all, he was responsible for his company writing some very large checks.

Every purchase for Austin, large or small, was a competition. It didn't matter if it were a bag of metal screws or a house; each required the same level of attention and exacerbating detail. He focused on making the very best purchase a person could make, which ultimately resulted in wearing down his opponent. He was relentless since he had time on his side and a checkbook in his pocket. He would no sooner part with a dollar in a frivolous manner than burn money to keep his home warm. I observed him over and over put out what he called his "RFP" (request for proposal) for everything from a dishwasher to a gutter replacement. Each time, he got multiple bids from various suppliers, and then he began his process of working them to "fight" for his business. He felt he was the only customer in his prospective suppliers' world and they were privileged even to be considered by him. Watching him was both enlightening and educating on all fronts. But I never agreed with his method because it was all one-sided. And that would of course be his side.

It's my belief you should not expect to have anyone provide a product or service for less than it costs to support it. You have to ask yourself, "How much money should you expect someone to lose for providing you with his or her services?" This doesn't mean you should take the first price that comes along and not do a competitive analysis. But having done your research and compared prices/benefits from various suppliers, you will be readily able to discern from your analysis a ballpark figure on where things stand. If someone comes in on either end of the pricing spectrum, one should definitely be suspicious and inquire as to why the extreme delta in pricing. That is when the sale begins. If the supplier is good and can explain specifically the difference in benefits and features, you'll understand very quickly the variation. If not, you're bound to choose the lesser-cost supplier for the options before you.

In Austin's case, he sought to find the lowest bidder on every occasion. And once he found that poor schmuck, he pounded on him to lower the price even more. In most situations I witnessed, he got exactly (and many times less) than what he paid for. It's just the way things work.

My experience has always taught me to do my homework, and in so doing, take the time to understand what the supplier is supplying. That's as important in a negotiation as knowing how much you have to spend or how much you can sell your product or service for to make a profit. It's not about "winning" or "beating" your adversary. It's about ensuring you'll have someone you can and want to work with again and again. The world is just too small to view it any differently whether you're on the buying or the selling side of the equation. Setting your goals on creating a win-win outcome for your suppliers and clients will pay you a lifetime annuity and make for an Extraordinary Life.

Finding satisfaction in work is our best hope for happiness in life.
— **Gandhi**

"SELLING IT" WHILE NOT "MISSING IT"

18 Execution Tips, plus 1 Bonus Tip, for "Selling It" in an Extraordinary Life, while not losing your "Balance."

1. **Accept Failure:** You cannot get better unless you allow yourself to fail. It is not about how many times you fail; it's about how many times you get back up after you have failed that makes for mastering an Extraordinary Life! Each time you fall short, you learn something. Look upon failure as a gift to your future success!

2. **Stop worrying:** Pay little attention to what others think about you. You will be paralyzed in your efforts if you listen to what others think you should do. Criticizing others is the favorite pastime of those afraid to live an Extraordinary Life.

3. **Get a Life:** Without one, it is difficult to enjoy building your life. And no one is interested in buying anything from "wallpaper," including buying wallpaper! "Getting a Life" is crucial for you to experience a balanced existence. If you are all work and no play...it makes for misery day after day! Diversifying your life creates a structure that allows you not to suffer great falls. "Getting a Life" helps you take the time needed to replenish your being, to open

up your scope to see a bigger picture—the totality of your life as a complete entity. The richer you make all aspects of your life, the richer you will be spiritually, emotionally, and financially.

4. **Mindset:** Train your MIND to SET you free. Reframe your thinking. Mastering your Extraordinary Life, including your financial and emotional success, depends on the stuff that goes on in-between your ears. The key principle in creating an Extraordinary Life lies within your thinking. If you think you can, then you can. Choose to develop a mindset for an engaged life that brims with a can-do attitude! Don't let yourself or others dictate your success. Your belief in your abilities will train your mind to set you free!

5. **Passion:** You spend approximately 84,000 hours of your life at work. Maintaining a high level of passion is the secret to job security and job satisfaction. Make the choice to trust yourself and follow your passion, but be smart about it. In order to live your Extraordinary Life, you need to maintain your means to feed your passion. When people display their passion, it becomes infectious and leads to great profit financially, emotionally, and spiritually!

6. **Visualization:** You need to see what Mastering your Extraordinary Life looks like before you can create the course for how you get there. Visualization is the key for turning your dreams into reality. If you can see it, you can create it! Build a Vision Board and visit your "success vision" daily.

7. **Motivation:** Surround yourself with interesting and positive people, professional coaching, and an empowering mentor. Motivate yourself with an intravenous feed of motivational books, tapes, webinars, podcasts, art, music, seminars, and mastermind groups.

8. **Taking Action:** Create a plan, write it down, and work it daily! Real progress comes from engaging in a full life that includes hitting your success milestones and professional goals. Without Taking Action, you can't reach your goals. You can't hit a hole-in-one if you never take a swing at the ball. Start everyday with a big fearless giant action step. This tip will build upon itself if worked daily, making each day more Extraordinary. Doctor's orders—one action a day will keep the competitors away!

9. **Attitude of Gratitude:** Being grateful and learning to live as if you have cancer brings a healthy dose of gratitude to all things important and brings richness to each and every day. It will help you define success, by identifying what makes you most grateful. Living an Extraordinary Life filled with gratitude will help insure that your priorities align with what makes you grateful.

10. **Community:** Seek out the foundation of likeminded people. Connecting to a community will add growth to your bottom line and emotionally support you when you lose your hairline! Giving back and being a part of something larger than you offers an extraordinarily powerful connection. When participating in a community (spiritual, social, civic, or professional), always build lots of bridges and never burn any of them!

11. **Patience:** Living an Extraordinary Life, manifesting your dreams, and holding yourself accountable to live each day as extraordinary takes a great deal of time and patience. Be extra mindful during dips in the economy and a "rocky market." Trust that in time and with constant execution, the fruit of your efforts will be yours for the picking!

12. **Accountability:** Measure outcomes. In order to achieve consistent progress in reaching your desired results/goals, no better formula will keep you accountable.

13. **Perseverance:** Never give up, no matter who tries to discourage you. You can enjoy your Extraordinary Life no matter where you are in achieving your ultimate goals. Make a pact with yourself to turn a blind eye to naysayers. Take pride in your ability to actualize the daily steps toward your progress. Think like The Little Engine That Could—it's not just kid stuff...achievers in life ride that principle, "I think I can, I think I can" all the way to their emotional, spiritual, and financial banks!

14. **Preparation:** Do your homework and be prepared from every angle. Doing your "homework" will help you maintain a high level of confidence. What level of trust will your readiness bring to the table? Your preparation creates an environment, an atmosphere for you to relax and participate in reaching your objective. Whether it is getting a good night's sleep, researching the prospect or competitor, or practicing your presentation to the point of delirium, "doing your homework" allows you to bring home an extraordinary report card!

15. **Extraordinary Listening:** Along with doing your homework, developing your ability to be a really good listener cannot be understated. Recall you were given two ears and one mouth...think about it! Therefore, feel your confidence and ask your prospects and partners what they need to have done to fix any problem. If you confidently ask and fully listen to the respondent, much of the hard work will be accomplished because you'll be given strategies for filling a gap or solving any problem. You walk away the hero for having provided a platform of understanding and now you have increased resolutions for your customer or prospects. Be an extraordinary listener and most of your headaches, backaches and neck-aches will vanish.

16. **Internal Compass:** Listen to your mind, body, and soul along the way. These are your "internal coaches" and they are a good barometer for maintaining your authenticity toward your desired Extraordinary Life and individual goals. Remember, you're working to reach your personal desires, not just to win. If you're in it just for the win, you will be left feeling empty after much sacrifice and hard work.

17. **No Excuses:** Make your choices and leave excuses behind. This does not mean being harsh or judgmental; it just means stopping the pattern of negativity that is getting in the way of Mastering an Extraordinary Life. It's not enough to "do the best you can." Grab the controls and take control of your life.

18. **Have Fun:** My favorite tip—enjoy the ride and have ridiculous amounts of fun. If you are not having fun on a

regular basis, it's time to reevaluate your values and goals. It's your life...get an "E" for Extraordinary ticket, and then, "Ride, baby; ride!"

BONUS TIP

- **JUST BE**—This overriding tip is paramount. Build in time just to be! Just stop! If you don't...life will stop you! If you don't take time routinely to stop rushing, stop the noise, stop the race, you run the risk of losing yourself on your journey. Learn to breathe, to be still with your thoughts, just to be.

- Those who succeed find creative ways to get what they want. Others who are not successful choose to spend time trying to convince the world why they were not able to achieve goals or personal happiness. Only you can devote the required degree of thought to embracing each learning experience, any obstacles, all victories, both big and small, as Extraordinary building blocks. Making a commitment to your persistent no-excuse attitude will serve you well. It makes for Extraordinary days, and it provides you with insurance to avoid the "blame game," which gets you nowhere and nothing.

- Continually moving yourself forward regardless of your deficits (we all have them, so what) is essential. Life is rarely fluid, but learning to incorporate these key tips for your desired success, including sales (you always have to sell someone on something in life) will increase your capacity for living your Extraordinary Life in the moment, as you soar!

Chapter 15

MAKING YOUR DAY EXTRAORDINARY

IT'S THE SIMPLE THINGS IN LIFE THAT ARE THE MOST

EXTRAORDINARY.

– PAULO COELHO

Recently I reached out to my family, friends, and business associates to ask each person *five* things that would make his or her day "extraordinary." What an interesting experiment it turned out to be! The answers not only shed an amazing insight for me into the individuals who responded, but my reply rate was nearly 80%. Clearly, my request struck a chord. It's been so long since I got an 80% response to anything that it was beyond my comprehension.

Before I requested the input, in a stream-of-consciousness manner, I wrote out approximately one hundred items I felt would make for an extraordinary day. All were items in my control, such as: giving my kids an extra hug, telling them how much they mean to me, talking to a complete stranger, giving someone an unsolicited compliment, writing a story, getting a facial, sending snail mail to friends expressing my feelings for them, going to Costco, etc. It was a great exercise, and it's now something I return to anytime I'm feeling a bit on the dark side of the moon.

Having taken the time to write down these self-fulfilling prophecies and give them a sprinkling of meaningful consideration, the next day I set out to see exactly how my thoughts would make for an extraordinary experience. An outing to Costco was eminent since I needed several household items that only Costco has been able to satisfy for the past several years. Off I went. And as I stated on my list, a visit to Costco makes for an Extraordinary day. Call me simple (and maybe a bit sick) but I must say, I love the experience of going to Costco. It's my favorite place on the planet to shop. And I'm not a shopper!

As I strolled the aisles, I was very cognizant of all the people, sights, and sounds around me. More so than I can ever recall being before. I was on the lookout for people to talk to, new items to see on the shelf, something pleasant to observe, and to say hello or just give a passerby a warm and hearty smile from a happy and content fellow Costco shopper. I filled my cart with the provisions I sought as well as a few items I absolutely didn't need (this felt really good and Costco loves shoppers like me for it).

When it came time to checkout, I decided to get into the line that was the longest and had the people with the most "stuff" in their carts. That way, I figured I would prolong my experience of having an Extraordinary day. As I approached the counter, I noticed the young woman behind the register wearing matching eye shadow to complement her pink and white-striped blouse. You could tell that making herself look good was not only part of her daily routine but a part of her persona in which she took great pride; after all, her pink blended in perfectly with her white and vice-versa.

I complimented her on her eye shadow and how she was so perfectly color-coordinated. This simple gesture absolutely lit her up like a Christmas tree from ear to ear, as well as the lady who was working side-by-side with her "boxing" up the goods. The latter said, "She's always like that; everyday she coordinates. Look at her shoes!" They both beamed and the checker told me "YOU JUST MADE MY DAY" and "Will you be back tomorrow? I want you to come through my check stand everyday."

Imagine that, eye shadow! Is it really that easy to make your day "Extraordinary"?

Chapter 16

MAKING YOUR DAY EXTRAORDINARY – PART II

THE MOST REVOLUTIONARY ACT WE CAN COMMIT IN THE
WORLD IS TO BE HAPPY.
— PATCH ADAMS

The other day I witnessed an all too often occurrence—a public display of customer dissatisfaction. When I say all too often, I mean that I don't believe these occurrences have to happen at all. We have all at one time or another not received the level of service we wanted or deserved. It's part of life and bound to happen. However, there are also proper ways to handle a situation of "perceived wrongdoing" and also inappropriate ways to handle it. I had the misfortune of witnessing the latter, and when that happens, it has the opposite effect of brightening my world.

I was at the local carwash waiting in line to pay my bill while my car was traveling down the washing assembly line. A man in his late fifties stormed into the store from the waiting area, cut in line, and demanded to "speak" to the manager. The man was so filled with rage he was like a tiger trapped in a net. The cashier, looking up from her task at hand, asked, "Would you like to speak with the store manager or the wash manager?" "I don't care which," he retorted. "Whichever one is going to give me my money back. I just spent twenty-three dollars for the worst car wash I've ever received. The windows weren't cleaned, the carpets not vacuumed, and there's still smudge on the wheels. This is without a doubt the worst carwash I've ever had in my entire life, and I demand you give me my money back!" His outburst made everyone in the building uncomfortable because he was completely out of control, and his explosion was way over the top for the minor mishap he had experienced. Had someone purposely dropped a boulder on his car and crushed his dog inside, perhaps his reaction and flare-up would have been on target. But not for something that could easily be rectified by rewashing his windows, running a vacuum cleaner, and polishing the wheels.

The man went on and on about how he'd been wronged, how the carwash misrepresented its service, and how he DEMANDED his money back. The red-faced cashier did her best to pacify the raging beast, but he was not to be appeased. No, he was hell-bent on making everyone around him know he was an angry bear not to be trifled with. Even after he was given his recompense, he continued to growl his level of discontent by swearing at the unsuspecting attendant who handed over his car with a smile (that beckoned a forthcoming tip). After all, the latter was not privy to the tirade inside the shop. He was quickly enlightened.

Traffic passing by the parking lot was heavy at the time the man was ready to depart. So much so that he had to sit for a good two or three minutes and stew in his own mess while waiting for an opening in the traffic flow so he could pull out in his scratched and dented '80s-something SUV. I thought to myself while he spewed red, doing his best not to make any kind of eye contact, there certainly is a God.

Once the irate man finally made his departure, I couldn't help but wonder how many times a day he pulled a similar stunt. It seemed obvious to me as the innocent bystander that this was a way of life for this sad and unhappy individual. To think, all that ill will and bad energy just to receive a free car wash.

Later that day, I was scheduled to get a facial, one of my favorite activities that help to make for a day *extraordinaire*. I was looking forward to it as I definitely could use a different perspective following "calamity at the car wash."

I went to my favorite pedicure spot because I had decided I would give the staff there a shot at a facial—a first for me at this location because the shop is designed primarily for nails (but does advertise additional spa services). The shop is worked entirely by women, mostly Philippine and Vietnamese, who are all in their twenties and early thirties and work ten to twelve-hour days six days a week. And I mean WORK. One client after another. And they also have to commute an hour or so each way because they cannot afford to live close by.

The girl who gave me my facial didn't know tips from toes, let alone a face. She happens to be disabled (my guess polio). She is very sweet and does her utmost best, but I'm afraid she wouldn't know a professional facial if it reached up and bit her in the butt. Because of her handicap, she has to exert more effort than her coworkers because it's very hard for her to maneuver between the tables, chairs, and the nail carts dragging her non-working leg. It's always nice to see the others pitch in wherever possible to help her in a tight space. They all do it subconsciously without a single spoken word or sign of contempt.

As I lay there uncomfortably receiving a facial massacre, I thought about what had transpired earlier at the car wash. It was obvious; God was putting me to the test. So I made the conscious decision to focus on her doing her level-headed best to ensure an enjoyable experience for me, and NOT on her inability to perform successfully the task at hand. She asked several times throughout about my comfort zone, and what if anything more she might do to improve it. Bless her heart—she wanted so much to make my experience pleasurable.

Had I continued to focus on her ineptitude, I am certain I would have resorted to having a miserable time, and I would have left completely irritated and dissatisfied, similar to the screaming banshee I'd witnessed just hours before. By shifting my focus to one of "let it go" and "let it be what it is" I really opened some doors for me. After all, let's weigh the other options: get up, walk out, yell and scream, criticize her, and refuse to pay? Yes, I could have chosen any of those alternatives. But in my moment of choice, I asked myself, "Will any of those alternatives make for an Extraordinary day?" The resounding answer was "I highly doubt it." It certainly wouldn't have made hers.

When she finished, she smiled broadly and asked me three questions: "Did I like the foot massage? Did I like the warm hand wrap? Did I like the way she massaged under my neck?" The answer to this round of questioning was a resounding "YES" as I DID like all those aspects of the hour long treatment. Who wouldn't? It doesn't get much better than having another person rubbing your feet, hands, and neck with warm oil, does it? She in fact had made my day Extraordinary.

Life is about choices. We either choose to enjoy life or we choose to complain about it. As I say, had I chosen the latter, my day would not have been Extraordinary. Shifting my internal focus made it so. With the help of those around me (yes, even the carwash curmudgeon), my eyes have been open to living an Extraordinary Life everyday.

CHOOSING EXTRAORDINARY

I have reverse paranoia; I always think people like me.
— **Aunt Dottie**

How you spend your time is a reflection of what makes up your life. If you want a more connected relationship with your children, you need to do something to connect to your children. If you want to live a healthier lifestyle, you need to do something to be healthier. If you want to have more satisfaction in your job, time for yourself, your hobbies, your life, you need to do something that will reflect it. In other words, if you want to create an Extraordinary Life, one that surpasses the ordinary, you need to choose to do something that embodies that, if only to begin with a shift in your consciousness.

Choosing to see what is Extraordinary in you and in your life helps to lift you up and a reflection of Life as Extraordinary begins to emerge. Gratitude for the "ordinary" becomes the Extraordinary. Miraculously this principle is true, even in the midst of facing life's most difficult challenges. We choose the tenor of our lives by being aware that although much may be out of our control (including cancer and life's "cancerous situations") we get to choose our actions and responses. Simply, we decide our perspective, so why not choose to see all that is Extraordinary in Life.

Viktor Frankl M.D., PhD., the acclaimed bestselling author of *Man's Search for Meaning* (named one of the ten best books of all time by the Library of Congress), was an Austrian neurologist and psychiatrist and a Holocaust survivor who knew all too well the value of choosing your mindset as he famously said:

Everything can be taken from a man but one thing: the last of the human freedoms—to choose one's attitude in any given set of circumstances, to choose one's own way.

Choosing to see Life as Extraordinary is an important Mastery Method. It lends itself to helping us all to be fully present to "Not Miss It" and to enjoy the blessing of each moment in the now.

In addition, seeing your life as an evolutionary process, a journey, empowers you to take the actions needed to settle into your "own skin," forgive others, and accept yourself as the Extraordinary being you were born to be. Life's tests, and the lessons that need to be learned along the way, are often gifts in disguise; they help us to reach the height of our growth process, and they lead to futures that are sure to unfold and be revered as Extraordinary Lives. We become people who rarely "Missed it"!

MASTERY QUESTIONS

What are situations in your life currently that you find challenging, frustrating, upsetting, or that you would rather avoid?

_____

_____

For each one, how can you improve your attitude or shift your thinking toward the situation and then potentially change it?

_____

_____

Chapter 17

COUNTING
YOUR BLESSINGS

GOD GAVE YOU A GIFT OF 86,400 SECONDS TODAY.
HAVE YOU USED ONE TO SAY "THANK YOU?"
— WILLIAM ARTHUR WARD

As you've read through these chapters, hopefully I've made it clear that I've led a very blessed life. It was not by accident since I feel I've had nothing but help from others in my life along the way. That is one of the biggest blessings of them all.

To illustrate this point, upon finishing my final week of cancer treatment, which can be described as nothing other than a marathon of chemo and radiation therapy, I meditated on what I had gone through and survived.

One key ingredient during this tenuous time that helped me immensely was the time spent with my family and friends. I made a concerted effort to have lunch/dinner, go for a walk, visit a museum or the market, have tea, etc. each day of treatment with good friends and family members.

This time spent with close friends was a true blessing that

reminds me again how fortunate I am to have the people in my life that I do. It's very special indeed!

On the top of my blessing list is my parents. I meditate over and over on how much they mean to me and how incredible they have been to me over the years. They helped form the very fabric of who I am as a person. I always thank God that they are who they are and how fortunate I am to have them as the key and guiding light through my journey on earth.

During one of my meditative prayers, I felt God say to me that I was able to pick my folks in Heaven before I came to live on earth. I'd had many people to choose from, so I had to pick well because they would be the only parents I would ever have. I was not given a window on the future, only to look at them as humans and how they acted as people on earth. My parents would be my decision to pick, not the other way around. So depending upon the life I wanted to lead on earth would determine a lot about how I made this decision.

Needless to say, this understanding was a true revelation and one that became dogma throughout my meditations. It opened all kinds of thoughts and self-observations, and ultimately, it put more accountability on me regarding who I am and how I live my life—a life without room for blame or self-criticism. It was truly a BLESSING to come to this realization, and one I doubt I ever would have come to had I not gone through several weeks of hell.

I highly recommend taking a moment from your day to meditate upon your blessings. You may be pleasantly surprised what comes before you. I know I was.

As an exercise, I recommend you take the time to write down the multitude of blessings in your life—one blessing at a time. There's no telling the possibilities that will open up for you. Here are just a handful of mine:

- I am blessed because I have chosen life in lieu of the alternative.

- I am blessed because I have God on my side.

- I am blessed because I have two amazing children who love me and I love them.

- I am blessed because I have the parents I chose.

- I am blessed because of the many friends I have to call my friends.

- I am blessed because I've done exactly what I wanted to do in my life.

- I am blessed because I've never missed a meal.

- I am blessed because I paid myself first.

- I am blessed because I've always lived in a home instead of just a house.

- I am blessed because I've seen so many wonderful things this world has to offer.

- I am blessed because I have the freedom to make a choice.

- I am blessed because there is no one else exactly like me.

- I am blessed because I chose cancer opposed to the other way around.

- I am blessed for being given a second chance at life, being awakened, and living an Extraordinary Life.

I am blessed because… well, you can take it from here…

FIGHTING IT

CANCER IS A WORD, NOT A SENTENCE.
— JOHN DIAMOND

Whenever my good friend Greg was having a challenge in his life, he'd walk into my room or give me a call and inform me he was "Fighting it." Greg is from Alabama and stands about six foot six in his socks. With a deep baritone voice that can only come from the depth of a man that size, when he'd utter those words, it had meaning and you knew something was up. He'd state, "I'm in the middle of something I can't quite figure out, and I'm *fighting it*, Randy." I always thought this a very descriptive phrase because it clearly summed up a challenge in two very succinct words. To this day, I can always hear Greg's strong voice summon up the beast.

I am a big fan of Charles M. Russell, the Montana cowboy artist of the last century. Years after I was initiated into Greg's phrase, I read Mr. Russell's memoirs. He was a stickler for detail in his work, and when he couldn't get a charging buffalo or a cowboy's lariat to look the way it does in life, he would state, "I'm fighting it." Same meaning, different person.

I have since used this catchy phrase many times in my life when something wasn't going the way I expected or when it presented a test.

The other day, I was watching the evening news when the anchor announced that a famous movie director had died. He had been seventy some years old and had lost his "fight" with cancer. I have heard the expression "fight" in regards to cancer many times, but I had never paid much attention to it until I was myself diagnosed with cancer. I always thought that someone "lost" the battle, as many do with a terminal disease, and passed on. With the shoe now on my other foot, I have acquired a new understanding of this term.

I don't believe in *fighting* cancer the way people usually describe it. They like to say things like, "He's in the fight of his life" or "He's in the midst of a major battle to win the fight against cancer." To me, to "fight" connotes a struggle, to wrestle, disagree, combat, brawl, go to war, come to blows, etc. None of these terms are positive in my opinion—they only present negative thoughts in and around having a disease that strives to kill its host. Therefore, I prefer to "choose" cancer over it choosing me, and I work with it rather than fight it. This view might seem like semantics, but I believe a little reverse psychology is what's needed to work on what those nasty little cells are attempting to do inside one's body. I prefer to live with it opposed to fighting it and thus walking through life viewing it as a struggle. Having cancer does not require effort if you break the disease down to its lowest form. It's in me, but it's a part of who I am and I can live with it, not be at odds and fight against it.

I don't mean that having a good fight in one's life is a bad thing. I love a good fight—especially if it's competing for business or shooting a good round of golf and tackling the course. That's a good fight to engage in, and I welcome the onslaught. But to have to "fight" for my life because a bug has entered my body just doesn't seem on par with the pleasure of a good fight.

As I've stated, many blessings come with having cancer. Am I glad I got it and get to live with it? Not particularly. But one in three people in this country will "get" cancer in their lifetimes. Those are the statistics in today's health census. The sooner one begins to think in terms of living with cancer as opposed to fighting against it, the quicker those numbers will change. At least that's my thesis on the subject. Live life as if you have cancer and perhaps you'll remain one of the lucky ones who will never have to find out.

ACKNOWLEDGMENTS

We would like to acknowledge Emily and Riley Broad, and Sasha, Eli and Jonathan Rosen for their extraordinary love and eternal support!

ABOUT THE AUTHORS

RANDALL BROAD

Randall Broad is an entrepreneur, business founder, and the guiding force behind several successful enterprises. After working as a salesman in the aerospace industry, he moved to Hollywood to embrace his dream of being an actor, making several commercials and being employed as a leading man stunt double.

In 1985, after he returned home to the Seattle area, Randall Broad founded Opal Enterprises, a marketing services company focused on maximizing client resources by building and managing successful partner integration programs.

A cancer survivor, Randall Broad now takes the stage professionally to share his views and lessons on living a work/life balanced existence. When he's not speaking or working with clients, he enjoys investing in real estate and exploring the world with his two children. In It's an Extraordinary Life, he has chronicled his experiences and adventures for future generations to learn from and enjoy. He lives in Kirkland, WA with his son and daughter, Riley and Emily.

JUNE GRUSHKA-ROSEN, M.ED

June Grushka-Rosen, M.Ed. is an author, speaker, and the founder of ExtraordinarYou a Professional and Personal Development Coaching business that operates its services nationally. June's business, ExtraordinarYou, coaches individuals, business professionals, organizations, and corporations to "wake up" to what is most important and begin living extraordinary lives filled with balance, passion, purpose, and achievement.

Taking a circuitous route from mental health therapist to coaching, June has found her life's passion in helping other find or enrich their path as well. Through this book, she is fulfilling a vision of being able to reach a wide audience with her work.

Ms. Grushka-Rosen holds a Masters of Education in Counseling Psychology. She enjoys serving as an Advisory Board member and as adjunct faculty for Rutgers University's Small Business Development Center.

June resides in the Philadelphia area with her husband and two children.